AF583677

THE NEW
PLATFORM PAPERS

From the Heart

The Voice, the Arts and Australian Identity

VOLUME 2
December 2022

Julian Meyrick
GENERAL EDITOR

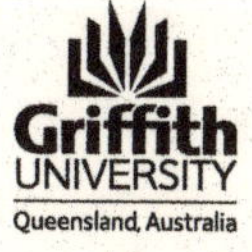

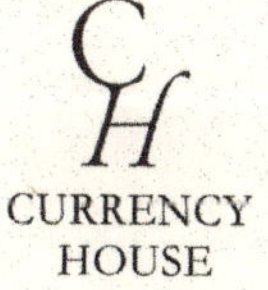

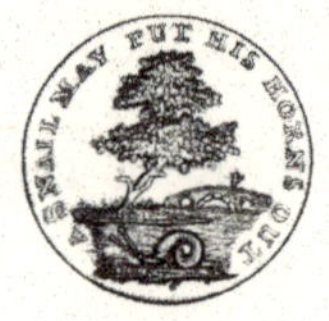

A snail may put his horns out

Thomas Spence (1750–1814) was an English radical who campaigned against private ownership of land. He argued instead for a system of democratic parishes. He was also a passionate believer in equality between the sexes. He was particularly active in the 1790s when he produced a radical magazine, *Pig Meat, or Lessons for the Swinish Multitude* from his book shop in High Holborn, London. He also produced a series of tokens, many of which carry radical messages. Some of these were overt—one bore an image of William Pitt the Younger's head stuck on a maypole surrounded by dancing revellers. Others, however, were more subtle. He was fond of combining animals with political slogans. 'A Snail May Put His Horns Out' was a reminder that even the most powerless have the ability to effect change through resistance.

Contents

Foreword, Julian Meyrick ix

Season's Greetings from Katharine Brisbane xix

No 2. *Arts, Culture and Country*

'Arts, Culture and Country'
Josephine Caust 1

'The Trouble with this Canoe'
Tyson Yunkaporta 51

'*J'accuse:* Australia's great crime against the jobless. The creation and perpetuation of the passive welfare underclass and the urgent need for a universal job guarantee.'
Noel Pearson 67

About the Authors 89

No 3. *From the Heart: the imperative for the arts~ the sector responds* 91

Introduction 93

'The Meaningful Expression of Indigenous Sovereignty through the Uluru Statement from the Heart'
Eddie Synot 97

'Art, Culture and the Voice'
Sally Scales 107

'Re-RIGHT-ing the Narrative'
Rachael Maza 117

'Power, Culture and the Search for Legitimacy'
Liza-Mare Syron and Harriet Parsons. 127

Contributors 132

No 40. *Take Me to Your Leader: the dilemma of cultural leadership* (reprinted)
Wesely Enoch 135

Submission to the Government on the National Cultural Policy
Currency House Board and Editorial Committee 207

List of Platform Papers 215

Julian Meyrick, General Editor

Julian Meyrick is a leading Australian theatre director and Professor of Creative Arts at Griffith University. His research focuses on the problem of value and evaluation processes in arts and culture.

Harriet Parsons, Director

Harriet Parsons took over the directorship of Currency House from her mother, Katharine Brisbane, in 2021. She is a contemporary artist and independent researcher specialising in the intellectual history of artistic practice.

Katharine Brisbane, Patron

Katharine Brisbane was the national theatre critic of the *Australian* from 1967 to 1974, a time of radical change. In 1971 she co-founded Currency Press, Australia's leading performing arts publisher, with her late husband, Dr Philip Parsons. Upon her retirement in 2001, she founded Currency House Inc., a not-for-profit association for promoting the value of the performing arts and expanding its discourse in public life.

Stephen Sewell, Authors Group

Stephen Sewell is the founding convenor of the Currency House Authors Group, a discussion group for the authors of Platform Papers, their associates and friends of Currency House. He is one of Australia's most celebrated writers for theatre and film, a former chair of the Australian National Playwrights Centre and was the Head of Writing for Performance at NIDA for eight years.

*

The history of Thomas Spence was kindly provided by Professor Hamish Maxwell-Stewart.

Thanks

As ever, we are grateful to our donors for their continuing support:

Annual Donors (3 years)

Katharine Brisbane, AM
Elizabeth Butcher, AM
Sally Crawford
Penny Chapman
Wayne Harrison, AM
Harriet Parsons
Geoffrey Rush, AC
Maisy Stapleton
Caroline Verge
Rachel Ward, AM and
Bryan Brown, AM
Kim Williams, AM
Margaret Leask

2022 Donors

Larry Galbraith
Nick Herd
Robert Love, AM
Mrs Marie Meyrick
August Supple

And the many small donors who have supported our work throughout the year.

Special thanks

We also thank the many friends who have kindly shared their advice and expertise, the staff of Currency Press and our accountants, Quantiphy. Special thanks to Jo Caust for her patient forbearance through the trial-and-error of producing the first commissioned essay for the New Platform Papers, and Liza-Mare Syron for her help in bringing together the speakers for the 2022 Authors Convention and mediating a truly memorable discussion.

This volume has been published with the generous support of the University of Sydney, School of Art, Communication and English.

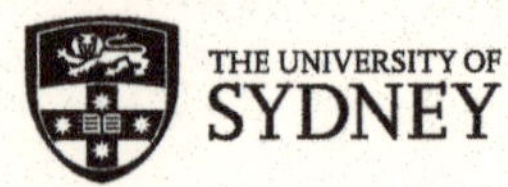

You need to suspend your disbelief that the nation can't change. You need to suspend your disbelief that Australia won't understand what you're trying to say. And we need you to imagine that the world can be a better place.

Professor Megan Davis[1]

1. Brianna Boecker, '"We seek a black voice": Professor Megan Davis and Pat Anderson on Voice to Parliament'. Women's Agenda. July 2022. womensagenda.com.au.

Foreword

Julian Meyrick
Yugarabul, Yuggera, Jagera and Turrbal country

Welcome to Volume 2 of the New Platform Papers with essays by Josephine Caust, Tyson Yunkaporta and Noel Pearson; the keynote speeches of Eddie Synot, Sally Scales and Rachael Maza from this year's Authors Convention, *From the Heart: the Imperative for the Arts*; Wesley Enoch's landmark essay from 2014 *Take Me to Your Leader* (reprinted); and the Currency House submission to the federal government on the National Cultural Policy consultation.

Such rich and diverse contributions demand introduction individually, but they are connected by the common thread of a concern for the distinctive place, role and value of First Nations in Australian life and culture. Sovereignty was to be the theme for the 2022 Authors Convention even before the election of a

Labor government in May ushered in a step-change in national priorities. The acceptance of the Uluru Statement from the Heart affects all areas of government policy, but it is especially significant for the arts.

In the National Cultural Policy consultation, the first goal those making submissions were asked to address was drawn from *Creative Australia*: to 'recognise, respect and celebrate the centrality of Aboriginal and Torres Strait Islander cultures to the uniqueness of Australian identity'[1]. It is the view of Currency House that this is not an *additional* policy goal but rather the gateway through which the vital question of 'Australianness' in our arts and culture should be properly understood. In other words, the full and free expression of First Nations culture is a matter that affects us all.

The essays in this volume bear this out in striking ways. They do not relay the same message or address the same topics—readers will note the authors' different experiences, outlooks and subject matters. Yet, taken together, they are a signal indication of the spiritual expansion that is taking place in our 'national imaginary' to include and own the real story of this continent, its First Nations and our modern Australian nation.

The implications for the future are momentous. It is becoming increasingly clear that a National Cultural Policy is about more than just the arts. Covid-19 has revealed that government programs have to do more than distribute a few, ever-shrinking arts grants to support our national culture. Affordable housing, higher wages, better social services are all key to a flourishing cultural sector *which is interconnected* with all other parts of our society and the economy. As Josephine Caust writes in the first essay of this volume, 'art, culture and country are one'.

In her essay, Caust explores the need to rethink the meaning of value in Australian arts and culture. Drawing inspiration, as well as practical lessons, from First Nations, she compares a worldview in which culture is considered central to a flourishing life, with the treatment meted out to the cultural sector during the Covid years of 2020–21—a sorry saga, full of neglect and slights. She makes a point that became obvious during successive lockdowns:

> Now, more than ever, the arts have become a part of our daily lives, no longer something only 'the elite' enjoy but an expression of an interconnected system of collective wellbeing... The arts reflect our whole culture, and our cultures are what make us who we are. When our culture is at the heart of our collective life, appropriate funding and support should naturally follow.

Caust has worked at almost every job in the arts. She has been a practitioner, producer, program manager, policy adviser and, today, researcher and cultural commentator. She reviews the one-step-forward-two-steps-back development of cultural policy in Australia since the 1970s. I urge everyone to read her essay because, whatever comes out of the current National Cultural Policy consultation, we must escape the deathly language this history has bequeathed us for evaluating everything in the cultural sector, from the smallest fringe theatre production to the largest billion-dollar streaming platform.

At the end of her essay, Caust puts forward the idea of a ministry of culture as a way out of what has often been a rudderless policy scenario. It is not a new idea, but what makes it timely is her call for a different philosophy to underpin it, one that takes its lead from First Nations to shape our culture's hierarchies, direct its processes and inform its actions more capaciously. To explore this philosophy, and how it might be expressed in policy terms, we publish two new works from First Nations authors. The first comes from the philosopher and artist, Tyson Yunkaporta, an astonishing and groundbreaking essay that leads the way in a uniquely Australian approach to cultural theory by integrating the intellectual history of Western philosophy with Indigenous methods of enquiry.

The second essay is the Renate Kamener Oration delivered by Noel Pearson at the University of Melbourne in March 2022, *J'Accuse: Australia's Great Crime Against the Jobless*. It is a passionate and authoritative call for a universal job guarantee.

In the past, Pearson has been a high-profile critic of passive welfare programs. He reluctantly accepted a 'natural rate of unemployment' that consigned 3-5% of the Australian population to outright poverty and a further 5% to exiguous under-employment, as a necessary evil. 'What is not admitted', he writes, 'is that our advantage sits directly atop this misery'.

It is worth recalling that in 1961, Sir Robert Menzies nearly lost office when unemployment topped just 2%. Today Indigenous Australians are over-represented in both categories. But there is no 'natural' unemployment rate. It is a false argument. The human pain and waste this nonsense credo causes is beyond calculation. Pearson's indignation is as compelling as it is searing:

> The political class knows that our social security system does an outstanding job of pacifying the excluded and the disadvantaged, by cutting off

> their hope and aspiration and giving them the false promise that their secondary services and programs will ameliorate their personal and social problems. And if not, then the tertiary services, in the form of end-stage medical care, out of home care for children and detention and incarceration facilities, can always be expanded.

Pearson's call is not just for a change to Australian economic policy, but the culture on which it is founded. His solution to poverty is for all Australians, but the potential benefits for Aboriginal and Torres Strait Islanders are proportionately greater, in line with their disadvantage:

> If we are going to close the gap, not only between Indigenous and non-Indigenous people but between the unemployed and the rest of Australia, we must ensure there are enough jobs for all those able to work and who want work.

Anthony Albanese's announcement that his government will implement the Uluru Statement from the Heart in full took the nation by surprise and sharpened the focus of this year's Authors Convention. We invited Eddie Synot, a constitutional lawyer, Sally Scales, a Pitjantjatjara artist—both members of the leadership team for the Uluru Statement reform—and Rachael Maza AM, Artistic Director of Ilbijerri Theatre, to consider what is required of Australian law and culture at this critical moment in our history. How might the Statement inform a National Cultural Policy and help bring it about?

So much damage has been done to First Nations culture since 1788, it is only natural that cultural policy should be central to the quest to implement the three elements of the Uluru Statement from the Heart: a Voice to Parliament, truth-telling and Makarrata. Modern Australia is a nation of immigrants, that is an indubitable social fact, but First Nations peoples are not just another minority group. As Eddie Synot writes, 'Indigenous interests are different: we are sovereign.' Sovereignty, he explains, is not defined in our constitution and means many things to many people. Each of the speakers considers what it *could* mean and importantly what we *need* it to mean as an institutional pillar of our culture.

For Sally Scales it means supporting Aboriginal arts centres in remote communities and legislation—with real penalties—to protect their artists from 'carpetbaggers'. She recounts shocking stories of modern-day slavery, of artists lured into exploitative contracts and forced to paint for unscrupulous art dealers:

> They might use a vulnerable family member to lure the artist into a debt... Then the carpetbagger might put up the artist in their home or pay for their hotel... At the same time, the first debt, from the original family member, also continues to grow. It is similar to the strategies used in sex slavery.

For Rachael Maza it means self-determination. 'Make space for us to be self-determined in our story making', she demands,

> because the stories that we will tell, will not be about dysfunction and how we all died out, but

> about our heroes, our resilience, our extraordinary sophistication and tenacity and political nous and phenomenally powerful communities. The point is, the stories that we will tell, will be our celebration of who we are. The stories that we will tell, will enrich this country. The stories that we will tell, we will share generously with this country, and this country will be the richer for it. And those are the stories that our kids will hear and be proud to be black.

All the speakers agree that if we are to come to proper awareness of the potential the future holds for our collective life, the rightful place of First Peoples, the oldest continuous living culture on this planet, must be acknowledged. Maza summed it up, 'Everything else flows from that.'

The aim of the New Platform Paper series is to equip policy-making with meaningful, grounded, professionally knowledgeable arguments and points of view. As such, it is important to bring back essays from the original series that still have things to say about current issues. In the 2021 volume we reprinted Platform Paper no. 63, *On the Lessons of History* by Katharine Brisbane, as an essay that was looking back over our past twenty years of publications as we were looking forward towards the future. Here, we reprint Platform Paper no. 40, *Take Me to Your Leader: the dilemma of cultural leadership* by Wesley Enoch from 2014. Enoch's essay is a perfect example of one that spoke to its time yet still resonates today. His demand that artists take on 'discussions of cultural change' was powerfully prescient. He put his main contention starkly:

> When was the last time you heard an artist talk about the state of the world? When have you seen an artist expressing anything that didn't seem self-interested or defensive?

At this year's Authors Convention, he got his wish. Artists came together with others to speak about the broader, structural factors that dominate our culture. In 2014, after Labor's *Creative Australia* had 'found the bottom of a bin' on the election of a new Coalition government, Enoch commented that 'whenever there is an attempt at a comprehensive [cultural] policy or leadership statement it seems doomed to be defeated by party politics'. It is to be sincerely hoped those times are now past.

Our submission to the National Cultural Policy consultation draws on many ideas from Currency House authors, and is reproduced at the end of this volume. We call for a Universal Job Guarantee that provides a minimum wage for recognised artists as the key to a flourishing cultural sector. We note this will have a proportionately greater impact on Aboriginal artists in remote regions by supporting the art centres that Sally Scales describes as the 'beating heart' of their communities:

> They are where our cultural advisors are, where intergenerational teaching happens, and they are also the place where artists have full control and autonomy over their income. They are the only place where artists can make something of their own that does not come from government... They are also the place where, if you are an elderly person or a person with a disability, you shine.

We call for a return to collegiality in the cultural sector's relationship with governments and policy processes. As Rachael Maza explains in her speech, the civility of courteous and inclusive listening leads to what Professor Megan Davis describes as a 'threshold of agreement'. This must underpin the Voice to Parliament, truth-telling and Makarrata, and without it they are meaningless:

> This is a way of working that is black-centred. That's not to say that we own it, but I believe that, as a way of making decisions, it is healthier than what we have at the moment, and in the Voice to Parliament, this country has an opportunity to learn from other ways of working.

Finally, we call for an end to 'the efficiency dividend', a false and counter-productive cost-saving measure that has become entrenched in government cultural expenditure budgets to the detriment of producers and consumers alike. It has long since outlived its usefulness and must go. As Caust rightly says, it is our artists who are the true embodiment of our national wealth.

The lesson of all these measures is that the foundation of a flourishing culture is the arts community, not its products. With this in mind, Currency House has sought to expand and nurture the discourse around the essays we publish, by encouraging further discussion. The introduction of the annual convention in 2021 was the first step towards this goal. We have also taken a new approach to our long essays by releasing them first on our website and publishing a revised draft in hard copy at the end of the year. This extends the debate and also allows us to publish and commission additional essays throughout the year that explore other dimensions of the author's idea. Josephine Caust's *Art, Culture and Country* was published on our website in March as the centrepiece of two discussions that were held at Currency House and Sydney University. It has been revised and updated after the election and the essays by Yunkaporta and Pearson take her ideas in new and exciting directions. We also published *Nobody Talks About Australianness on Our Screens* by Sandy George in June. We will be continuing the discussion of systemic problems in the film and television industry at events in 2023, and publishing her essay in its final form with related companion pieces in hard copy next year.

This year's Authors Convention marked the inaugural meeting of the Currency House Authors Group, a regular gathering of our authors, their guests and friends of Currency House, hosted by one of Australia's leading playwrights, Stephen Sewell. The meeting will be a place not only for discussion, but carrying new ideas forward into action. Through initiatives like these, Currency House seeks to support debate about Australian culture that embraces the spirit of the Statement from the Heart, and encourage artists who are willing, once more to debate the state of the world.

Endnotes

---

1. Simon Crean, *Creative Australia National Cultural Policy. Parliament of Australia*, 2013, p. 44. *Parliament of Australia*. www.aph.gov.au.

Season's Greetings

Dear Friends,

It has been an emotional year, 2022, our spirits alternately lifted and depressed by public and private events only tangentially connected. As for so many, the death of Queen Elizabeth II took my thoughts back to my own memories of her, in my case back to 1954 and her first royal tour of Australia. I was a cadet reporter on the *West Australian* and probably the member of staff they could most easily spare, so I was volunteered by the newspaper to sit in the back seat of a car and play her part for a rehearsal of the route she would be taking through the streets of Perth. As the years went by, I began to wonder if they had been looking for signs of Fenians. Irish Fenian interventions were not uncommon at the time.

In this country, the shadow of 1975 still hangs over Elizabeth's long, understated and generally popular reign, but Australians seem to be navigating their conflicting emotions with surprising ease and are showing generally positive feelings towards King Charles III. In past years, the speculation had been that this would be the turning point in our colonial relationship—that this would be the moment when the republican movement came into its own—but republicanism is taking a back seat during the period of mourning. Perhaps the pomp and ceremony televised from London helps—the extraordinary processions of military and civil officials in their ceremonial uniforms: the heralds, the Beefeaters, the Royal Guard, signal the endorsements of history as well as the people and the Parliament.

But the question of the republic is likely to continue to hold our attention, both socially and morally. The ceremonies now taking place in London that will be repeated by Governors General around the world, including ours, emphasise a thousand years of history. In this country we are only just starting to appreciate over 2,000 generations of living cultural heritage spanning more than 40,000 years.

Decades of neglect and harmful decisions have caused long-standing injuries to many in the wider population—women, low-paid workers, residents in aged care—that government is at last starting to redress. Their urgent needs that are being revealed by a growing number of crises must bring in reforms that will change our lives in ways we have not yet conceived. My guess is that within a decade the Universal Basic Income will be an established institution. But one reform of historic importance is closer to hand: the referendum on a First Nations Voice to Parliament. Prime Minister Anthony Albanese, whose way of getting things done is by consensus, is making the question easy for us. The referendum will simply ask, do we want this? And leave the details of the legislation to Parliament.

Moments like this—the birth of an Aboriginal and Torres Strait Islander Voice to Parliament; the death of a British monarch—expose the emotional power contained in an abstract concept that, until now, most Australians have been happy to pass off as an eccentric anachronism. But sovereignty is a serious issue for First Nations people and perhaps the death of Elizabeth II is not the moment we should be rushing on to a republic, but rather, a time to take pause and think about what sovereignty—the ermine and the possum-skin—means for us and our culture.

Wishing you all a joyous holiday season and every good prospect for 2023,

from Gadigal country.

Arts, Culture and Country

Josephine Caust

no. 2
March 2022

Acknowledgements

While I am the author of this work, I am drawing on the ideas and work of many other writers, commentators, artists and thinkers in this field. Firstly, I want to thank Julian Meyrick, Harriet Parsons, Ian Maxwell and Katharine Brisbane for their contribution to the development of this essay. I also want to mention several others and thank them for writing about and generously sharing their ideas with us all on this important subject. They include:

James McCaughey, Alison Carroll, Ben Eltham, Tully Barnett, Hilary Glow, Justin O'Connor, Alison Croggon, David Pledger, Wesley Enoch, Kate Fielding, Esther Anatolitis, Gina Fairley, Peter Tregear, Joanna Mendelssohn, Christiaan De Beukelaer, Guy Morrow, David Throsby, Donald Horne and Thomas Keneally.

***

This text was written on Kaurna Land. The author recognises the Kaurna people as the custodians of the Adelaide Plains. She also recognises the Indigenous custodians from other parts of Australia and overseas.

My background

This year marks my fifty years of employment in the arts. Over that time I have been an actor, artistic director, administrator, program coordinator, policy adviser, academic lecturer and researcher. And in the process I have also been witness to, and participated in, significant change across the sector.

My career began in 1972, straight after university, when I landed a job as a full-time actor at the South Australian Theatre Company. I was specifically employed for their festival production of Ben Jonson's *The Alchemist* directed by George Ogilvie. Of course, I didn't realise how lucky I was. There were only two female parts and around a dozen male. Later that year I went off to London to study acting and worked there in different theatre companies. The gender question, though, was always an issue and getting work as a female actor was much more challenging than for a male.

On returning to Australia in 1975 things were no better. I approached the then-artistic director of what is now the State Theatre Company of South Australia in Adelaide, George Ogilvie, for work. But the company was doing a season of all-male plays. (Odd, given that 1975 was the first United Nations International Year for Women.) So, in 1976, I moved to Sydney, acquired an agent and worked as a freelance actor. By late 1978 I had returned to London and was becoming disenchanted with the life of a 'jobbing' actor. I decided the time had come for a change of profession.

I took a job as the coordinator of a community arts centre in the South of London. This was run as a collective, which in turn challenged my own contradictory notions around leadership. Later I was accepted into the postgraduate program in arts administration at City University. Most of the lecturers were male while the majority of students were female. This encouraged a fellow student, Susan Feldman and myself, to develop a seminar series of guest lectures by women in the arts. The series morphed into the first National Conference of Women Theatre Directors and Administrators held in London in early 1980. A job as an administrator followed with the 7:84 theatre company, founded by the Scottish writer John McGrath. The name 7:84 and its repertoire reflected the reality in the UK of the late 1970s, where 7% of the population owned 84% of the wealth. But while the company had strong sympathy for the working classes, it still had no women employed as directors or writers. I raised this with John. Like many left-wing men of the time, he saw no contradiction.

So, in 1981 I accepted a job as a consultant in Sydney, as Director, Women and Arts in the Premier's Department of the New South Wales State Government under Neville Wran. The position involved organising a statewide Women and Arts Festival and coordinating a National Research Project (NRP). It was important to involve as many different voices in the festival as possible, so we had twelve advisory groups across a wide range of art forms and sectional interests. The NRP was funded by the

Australia Council and Gillian Appleton wrote a report for an Advisory Committee of senior women in the field. This research provided the first detailed data on women in the arts in Australia and was published in early 1983.

From there, I became a senior project officer on the Australia Council's Theatre Board, responsible for drama policy and funding nationally. The Council was starting to be squeezed financially by the Federal Government and more and more companies were competing for grants, so the Board sought a new solution to its burgeoning expenditure and introduced a 'ceiling' on funding that would limit the maximum amount awarded to individual companies to $300,000 per year.

The plan was not received well. At least half a dozen companies were already receiving much more than that. It became my role to communicate the new policy to the affected companies, and they in turn lobbied the incoming Labor government led by Bob Hawke. Their actions and Hawke's compliant response made me realise how political the relationship between government and the arts could be.

After a period working for arts organisations in Melbourne and Sydney, including the Victorian College of the Arts, I accepted the position of Director of Arts in the Arts Department of the South Australian Government. Economic rationalism was starting to have an impact in Australia and, although we tried to resist, assessment of arts activities based on productivity measures became entrenched.

In 1995 I returned to consultancy work. I worked for Asialink where I created the first residency schemes for Australian theatre artists and arts managers across Asia. I also undertook a consultancy with the University of Melbourne to design their new arts management program. In 1997 I joined the University of South Australia to direct their arts management program, completed a PhD in arts leadership and started the *Asia Pacific Journal of Arts and Cultural Management*. My place in the academic world succumbed to corporatisation when my Pro Vice-Chancellor suggested that arts programs were no longer economically viable.

Since 2011 I have been affiliated with the University of Melbourne as a Principal Fellow (Honorary) in the School of Culture and Communication. I have published widely on arts leadership and the sector, including a forthcoming book, *Governments and the Arts*. In what follows, I draw on all aspects of my professional experience to reflect on Australia's cultural policy history and make some proposals for the future. It is a narrative which is less well-known than it should be and deserves to be interrogated.

The reality of our times

When we think about art and culture in Australia, we must start with the First Nations peoples who have cared for the land on which modern Australians have 'settled' for thousands of years. For them, art, culture and country are entwined and interdependent.[1] Their wisdom and knowledge are a gift to the nation, and we should follow their example by respecting our nation's arts, culture and country as *one*. Caring for country, caring for culture and caring for the arts are inseparable. But traditional arts practices and languages are being lost every day through our neglect, greed and inattention, and the mining company Rio Tinto's wanton destruction of priceless Aboriginal cultural heritage at Juukan Gorge in 2020 shows how far we still have to go to achieve this holistic understanding.[2] If the cultural principles and aesthetic values we cherish are to be protected, they must be reflected in the policies and practices of government. The first step towards this change is to isolate the destructive beliefs and practices in our present culture that have brought us to our current position, so that we can consider how to address them.

The arts and the pandemic

The Coalition government's large-scale financial intervention to protect the community and prevent economic collapse at the height of the pandemic in 2020 was a revelation. Yet, while some sectors, such as aviation and construction, were given special treatment, others were pointedly left out of mainstream support programs.[3] One of these was the arts. The 2016 national census found that over 350,000 people were employed in the cultural sector, but Alison Pennington and Ben Eltham believe that this figure is an underestimate. They argued in a report for the Australia Institute in 2021, *Creativity in Crisis*, that it did not include the large number of artists who were employed in related businesses.[4] In 2018, the Federal Government itself calculated that the cultural and creative industries contributed A$111.7 billion to the Australian economy or 6.4% of GDP, and employed over 600,000 people.[5]

In mid-March, 2020, nearly all arts activity stopped. Theatres, galleries, arts centres, concert halls, cinemas and festivals closed. Film production ceased. Rehearsals were cut short and exhibitions were cancelled or went online. A website 'I Lost My Gig' was set up to track performing artists' loss of income and by the end of April more than $340 million had vanished from the sector.[6] This was a scenario that could not have been foreseen by artists. Most were already making a precarious living and few had savings to fall back on.[7]

The Federal Government under the Coalition pledged $27 million to support the sector: $7 million for Indigenous visual arts organisations, $10 million for regional artists and $10 million for the mental health service, Support Act.[8] It also provided general support through JobKeeper, a scheme that allowed employers to keep paying wages while business was restricted, and JobSeeker, a temporary unemployment benefit at an increased rate.[9] In April, the federal arts minister, Paul Fletcher, declared that most artists and arts workers were being supported by one of these two schemes.[10]

While it is true that some arts workers were able to access JobKeeper, many were ineligible because they were casuals or short-term contractors, and many in more permanent employment were treated as 'non-essential workers' by their own organisations.[11] On 19 March, for example, Opera Australia stood down its singers and orchestra without pay.[12] After wide public protest it reinstated them on half-pay and long service leave to May 2020, but a core administrative group of 35 staff, including all the company's senior executives, continued full-time, albeit on reduced salaries.[13] In early April, the Melbourne Symphony Orchestra then stood down its musicians.[14] The MSO members were eventually deemed eligible for JobKeeper but their treatment by their own management is troubling.[15]

Even receiving the JobSeeker unemployment benefit was difficult for many arts workers. For those who did apply, professions, like 'playwright' and 'visual artist' were simply not recognised categories of employment at Centrelink. Pennington and Eltham estimate that 53% of arts businesses closed after the first lockdowns in 2020, but while professional artists were losing their jobs, participation in the arts within the broader community increased, with two thirds of Australians seeking out arts activities.[16]

A report by Bill Browne, published by the Australia Institute in May 2021, calculates that if the Federal Government had invested $2 billion in the arts and entertainment sector instead of the construction industry in 2020–21, it would have created 8,593 jobs: *twice* as many jobs for men and *ten times* as many jobs for women. Women represent only 12% of the workforce in construction, while in arts and entertainment the gender balance is 49% men and 51% women.[17]

Over the first months of the pandemic it became clear that, despite the Federal Government's assertion that the critical factors determining its pandemic policy were economic, industries that employed many fewer people than the cultural and creative industries were receiving far more generous financial support. In particular, the 'private' sector businesses were being assisted while the 'public' sector was being ignored. Thus, private education providers were eligible for JobKeeper but public universities—the larger contributor to the economy with many more students—were not.[18]

In early 2020, the ABS revealed that 'arts and recreation' had been the sector hardest hit by the closures in Australia with 94% affected.[19] The Grattan Research Institute estimated that up to 26% of Australian workers were likely to lose their jobs due to lockdowns and restrictions, but in the creative and performing arts this figure jumped to a whopping 75%.[20] Yet Coalition politicians continued to portray the arts as a 'lifestyle' choice.[21] This was the harsh reality of 2020: arts organisations were suffering their greatest income loss in fifty years because of government measures to control the pandemic, but they were being excluded from government support.[22]

For months the Federal Government failed to address the impact the closures were having on the arts. For many this only proved that, however they were framed—as a common good or an economic driver—the Government neither valued nor understood the sector. It was not until late June 2020, after extensive industry lobbying, that the Government finally announced direct support for the sector. The main package, RISE, provided a fund of $75 million which it increased by another $125 million in March 2021, but applications did not open until September and the first approved grants did not arrive until November.[23] There were eight months in 2020 during which large parts of the arts sector received no federal support whatsoever to either re-start or plan activities for 2021.[24] The process also lacked transparency and it allowed room for political interference. Like George Brandis's National Programme for Excellence in the Arts[25] and Mitch Fifield's Catalyst Scheme that followed,[26] the minister made the final decisions on the RISE package arts funding, taking into account internal recommendations from government bureaucrats. The knowledge and experience of the arts sector does not seem to have been as important to this process as political priorities.

***

The impact of the pandemic on the Australian arts sector will be felt for years to come. While arts activities have re-started in most cities, the waves of Covid cases have created a climate of chronic uncertainty. The greatest impact was on Melbourne which experienced a total of 262 days of lockdowns in 2020–21. The Rising Arts Festival was cancelled after the opening night and Melbourne artists received little additional support from the Federal Government, despite their greater disadvantage. State governments were generally more responsive, offering emergency relief within weeks of the initial wave of closures, but their support was uneven and lacked a 'whole of sector' approach.[27]

The pandemic highlighted the *political and personal* priorities of both federal and state governments: major sporting events were supported while arts events were cancelled, sometimes at the last minute. Football teams were allowed to circumvent lockdowns and interstate border closures by staying in 'bubbles', but artists were rarely given the same opportunity. The 2020 Byron Bay Music Festival was cancelled before it had even opened, while only a few kilometres away neighbouring sports events continued. This all points to grounds for support that were anything but economic.

Australia is a wealthy nation?

The population of Australia has grown dramatically—in fact nearly doubled—since the 1970s, from 13.8 million to 25.4 million.[28] So has our GDP due to the mining boom of the 1980s. Even so, government funding for the arts has been continuously resisted, particularly at the political level, despite widespread support from the general community.[29] Instead of valuing our artists as the embodiment of our 'national wealth' and celebrating them, they have come to be treated as the 'deserving poor'. From

2008–18, the Federal Government actually *reduced* funding for arts and culture by 18.9% and by 2018 the proportion it spent on national culture at all levels had fallen from 45% to 39%. In 2015, Australia's contribution to culture was around .77% of GDP while the average of other OECD countries was 1.11%.[30] Despite its wealth, Australia spends less on culture than comparable nations and in 2017 was ranked 27th out of 33 OECD countries for its cultural expenditure.[31]

Since the 1970s Australia's demography has also been transformed by waves of immigration from Europe, Asia, the Middle East, Africa and the Americas. Our culture is not homogenous and there are as many arts practices here now as there are cultures. But while the amount of cultural activity has been increasing and becoming more diverse, arts funding has been steadily decreasing. Despite the many arts activities in outer suburban and regional areas, the largest proportion of arts funding goes to the 'European high arts' that are concentrated in the inner cities, skewing the distribution of funding both geographically and across practices and cultures.

This 'hierarchy' of cultures is well out of date. All citizens should have access to, and be able to participate in, the arts practices of their culture.[32] Australia is the only Western democracy that does not have a bill or charter of rights for its citizens, nor does it have human rights legislation embedded in its constitution.[33] A charter of cultural rights might ensure more equitable support for different arts practices and allow us to create policies that embrace all forms of cultural expression, accept their differences and celebrate them.

We also know that a regular income—a roof over our heads, food to eat—makes normal life possible and therefore provides *the means to contribute to society in a meaningful way.* In 1962, Donald Horne dubbed Australia 'the lucky country'. He was being ironic, but we can say that we are 'lucky' because our country is wealthy. If we measure the median wealth of adults on an international scale Australia comes out on top. In terms of mean wealth, we are fourth overall.[34] Certainly some Australians are very wealthy, but our wealth is not evenly distributed. The rate of poverty in Australia is worse than in many other wealthy countries and the gap between the haves and have nots has only widened over the years.[35] Today 13.6% of the population or 3.24 million people live below the poverty line.[36] The pandemic has seen other countries seriously considering—and even implementing—a universal basic income (UBI).[37] As a wealthy country, Australia could certainly afford to consider a scheme of this kind too. We could also afford to protect our culture and resources.[38] The continuous cycle of sustainable growth Kate Raworth proposes in *Doughnut Economics* curtails the trend that limits rewards to an ever decreasing few. Could Australia embrace this model and see arts and cultural production as a central part of a sustainable economic and social cycle?

The contradictions in our culture are immense. We lionise First Nations artists while their communities live in poverty. Their treatment is a matter of national shame. The official response to refugees fleeing oppression betrays a streak of xenophobia. Their plight has been exacerbated by climate change, yet in 2020, at a time when the world was trying to divest itself of its dependence upon fossil fuels, the Australian Federal Coalition Government provided $10.3 billion to the fossil fuel industry.[39]

Australia is out of step with the times. We need to learn to distinguish between profit and wealth and see our society and the environment as an integrated system in which everything is connected to everything else. When the interdependence of community and country is acknowledged, culture will naturally be located at the centre of our collective lives.

Wealth is reflected in all that we cherish, not our bank balances. Our First Nations are role models for cherishing our real wealth—our country and our culture—but we need to embed them in our legislation and our policies. When culture is cherished, so too are arts practices. We are in many ways a 'lucky country' but not in the way it is often understood.

Making a career as a professional artist is not easy. It requires enormous self-belief and resilience to overcome the challenges, obstacles and knocks along the way. The economist David Throsby and his colleagues have recorded the depressingly low incomes of Australian artists for many years. In their latest study in 2017, they noted that the average annual income from creative work was $18,800 and the average income for artists from all sources of employment was $48,400—21% below the workforce average.[40]

Professional artists are people who do their creative work because it is central to their being. Their work is a gift to the community, yet they are not treated as equals in our society. Why can't artists have access to all the normal social and economic benefits, without being slighted and demeaned? Why shouldn't they be able to access unemployment benefits while searching for work in their profession, as musicians, actors, artists and writers, as the rest of the workforce does? Why can't we institute fellowships for mid-career and senior artists that enable them to continue their work with dignity and respect? Treating the arts community this way requires a shift in attitude. It is in society's interest to acknowledge and respect our artists, our culture and its practices. It is part of who we are and connects us to our country. It is the real wealth of the nation.

Funding the arts: historical reflections

For the past thirty years, policymakers have framed the arts within an industry paradigm and made arguments to government based on their economic value. The shift to an industry model began in 1985, under Bob Hawke's Labor government, following an Inquiry into Commonwealth Assistance to the Arts that was chaired by Leo McLeay. The report from the House of Representatives Standing Committee on Expenditure, *Patronage, Power and the Muse* (the 'McLeay report'), was published in 1986, but there were several important policy events leading up to this moment.[41]

Before the mid-1980s funding for the arts had been justified as a 'public good': the arts were fundamental to a healthy society and should be made available to all.[42] This view had been inherited from the British economist John Maynard Keynes, who had been a powerful influence in the development of arts policy in the United Kingdom after World War II.[43] Keynes had also argued that deliberations should be conducted at 'arm's length' from ministers and the government of the day, so that decisions about funding were not influenced by party politics. This principle had underpinned the establishment of the Arts Council of Great Britain in 1946 and the Canada Council in 1957.

The Australian economist and senior public servant, Herbert 'Nugget' Coombs, who had studied under Keynes, was influenced by his approach and, through the 1960s, as governor of the Reserve Bank of Australia, worked hard to achieve bipartisan support for a similar model for arts funding here. Australia was relatively late in creating a statutory authority but, by the late 1960s, both sides of politics had come to favour this model. The Australia Council for the Arts did not become a formal statutory body until the Australia Council Act of 1975, but its mission was evident from 1973 when it began absorbing various existing bodies and by 1974 it was effectively operational. In establishing the Council, it was Prime Minister Gough Whitlam's assertion that 'In any civilised community the arts and associated amenities must occupy a central place'.[44]

The Council's mandate was to develop and support the arts across the nation as an essential facet of our national culture. In its first iteration it comprised seven boards whose government-appointed members were respected peers of the arts community and drawn from each art form. This was considered to be vital if the policies and programs of the Council were to be respected by artists themselves.[45] Importantly, Aboriginal Arts were recognised as a distinct art form with their own board. However, 1975, the year of the Australia Council Act, was also the year of the constitutional crisis in which the Whitlam government was dismissed, and the Council had hardly been established before, to borrow a metaphor from Ben Eltham, the goalposts were moved.[46]

Changing the model

In 1976 the Industries Assistance Commission (today's Productivity Commission) held an Inquiry into Assistance to the Performing Arts (the IAC Inquiry). It recommended phasing out funding for the major performing arts bodies over several years and that the sector begin operating as a commercial industry in the main.[47] The new prime minister, Malcolm Fraser, rejected the report and reaffirmed the government's commitment to subsidising the major performing arts organisations and all forms of arts practice. During Fraser's term of office, however, the chair and CEO of the Australia Council, Timothy Pascoe, observed that financial support decreased by 20%, leading to a 35% reduction in staffing.[48]

The relationship between the Australia Council and the government fundamentally changed when the Labor party, led by Bob Hawke, was voted into power again at an early election in 1984. The Council's Theatre and Music Boards were proposing to limit the amount that could be awarded to any one organisation so that their limited pools of funding could be distributed more widely to a growing number of artists.[49] The major performing arts organisations lobbied the government to block the changes. While Hawke did not overrule the Boards, he committed an additional $802,000 to the Australia Council which he earmarked for the large performing arts organisations. This direct political action undermined the authority of the Council by demonstrating to the major arts organisations that if they did not like a particular funding decision they could lobby ministers directly, scuttling the arms-length relationship between the Council and the government. The major companies continue to receive the lion's share of the Council's funding to this day, a share that has only increased as the Council's annual allocations have continued to fall.[50]

By the late 1980s, the ideology of economic rationalism (neoliberalism) had become the policy mantra of the Hawke

Government.[51] All government policies were to be framed in economic terms, public bodies privatised wherever possible and activities measured in terms of 'productivity' and 'efficiency'. Fraser had rejected the recommendations of the IAC inquiry in 1976 but now, ten years on, the Hawke Government was embracing them.[52] The McLeay report explicitly framed the arts in industry terms and although the arts resisted the change, the shift to economic rationalism was relentless.[53] Abandoning Keynes' notion of the 'public good' had an immediate impact on the arts that has had lasting effects.

Despite his prescient observation that 'no economic or social decision is without a cultural consequence' the shift only intensified under Prime Minister Paul Keating.[54] In 1994 Keating published Australia's first national cultural policy, *Creative Nation*. This document argued eloquently for the importance of culture in everyone's life, but revealingly the term 'arts' played only a minor role in the narrative. Instead, the 'creative industries' entered the language. It could be argued that the Labor Party pursued the industry model as a way of mainstreaming the arts sector and framing artists as legitimate workers, wrongfully under-resourced and undervalued, but the downside was that the arts were now required to become growth- and profit-driven corporate entities.

For policymakers and bureaucrats the 'arts industry' was a concept they could understand. There was no longer any need to worry about the tricky problem of evaluation: success meant how many people saw a theatre production or bought a CD or a book, or how many people a company employed. The arts could be measured by inputs and outputs instead of public benefit. This emphasis on numerical assessment provided a solid base for economic argument by demonstrating the income-earning potential of any form of arts practice. The ABS now includes design, fashion, broadcasting, electronic and digital media, film, libraries and archives, literature and print media, heritage, performing arts, visual arts and crafts, music composition and publishing, as well as other cultural goods and sales in its definition of the sector.[55] The creative industries had recast artistic practice as a commercial activity that generates growth and profit from production. The corollary of this model was that it implied that, if properly managed, this 'industry' should not rely on government support.

Many people involved in the newly-defined creative industries began to describe themselves as 'creatives'. The terms 'artist', 'arts worker', 'director', 'curator', 'producer', 'arts administrator' or 'arts manager' were gradually being replaced by the one generic term. But what does the title 'creative' actually mean? It is hard to say beyond that it implies that the individual has a connection with the 'creative industries'. Many professions require a degree of creative skill—a scientist, a road planner and an engineer could also be described as 'creative'. Is this a problem? Yes and no. As a term it might be well understood within the cultural sector, but it is less so further afield, because it does not convey what the actual work is that a creative person does. Perhaps it is useful for describing people who work in the media, where individuals use 'creative' thinking to solve industrial problems, but whether we would describe them as artists is up for debate.

The disappearance of 'artists' and the 'arts' from our language is deeply troubling. Both have fallen out of favour and become terms of casual dismissal, even abuse. Being 'a creative' is hip. Being 'an artist' is pretentious. Saying that you work in the 'arts' can be seen as elitist and old fashioned and a sign that you are out of touch: no longer part of the technical, post-modern world in which today's Australians live. Governments have consciously or unconsciously encouraged this negative perception by facilitating the demise of these words and the cultural history they carry with them.

Business entities

Paul Keating established a new entity in 1994 modelled on the US National Endowment for the Humanities. The Australian Foundation for Culture and the Humanities was located in Melbourne with a mission to address broader issues in Australia's history and cultural heritage. But once again, a change of government put an end to its cultural agenda.

John Howard's Coalition government was elected in 1996 in a landslide victory that few expected. In 1999 the Foundation for Culture and the Humanities morphed into the Australian Business Arts Foundation (ABAF) and its mission was repurposed to raise private sector support for the arts. It is now called Creative Partnerships Australia (CPA), but its mandate remains essentially the same: 'to find private sector support for the arts through partnerships, one-off and ongoing sponsorships, and philanthropic engagement'.[56] The establishment of the ABAF/CPA signalled the transition to the US model of private sector sponsorship as the preferred approach for funding the arts and direct funding was no longer seen as the way forward.

The Howard Government established the Major Performing Arts Organisations Board (MAPAB) on the recommendation of the Nugent Inquiry into the Major Performing Arts (the Nugent

Inquiry) in 1999.[57] As in 1984, the Council was unable to fund cultural organisations equally and this fenced-off the larger performing arts organisations from their smaller peers, so that they could be assessed on business rather than artistic criteria. MAPAB provided guaranteed funding through multi-year contracts. To be eligible the companies just had to be solvent. In the event, they did not even have to meet that criterion, as the Sydney Dance Company was rescued financially in early 2007 and a number of State opera companies also continued to trade while insolvent in 2016–18.[58]

The Coalition's managerialist approach to policy implied that if cultural organisations were operating properly 'as businesses', they would need minimal government support. Perhaps it was imagined that direct federal funding would eventually cease all together, save for a few favoured groups based on western cultural heritage norms that were essential to the national identity: a national gallery, a national museum, a national library, a national opera company, a national ballet company and a national theatre company. Other organisations would either be supported by State and local governments or become self-sufficient. The idea of arts companies as corporations took hold and the language of business plans, performance indicators and strategic development was embraced.

During this period the ratio of 80% subsidy to 20% earned income reversed. For the major performing arts companies in particular, this meant that they had to start prioritising box office income over artistic risk.[59] This financial change was accompanied by a new determination that the boards of arts companies should be populated by people from the business sector, who knew how the 'real world' worked and could teach artists how to be 'businesspeople'. These new board members did not need to know anything about the arts. In fact, it was considered an advantage if they did not, as they were less likely to be 'captured' by the artists. They would work on generating new sources of income from the private sector and curtail those activities they judged to be indulgent, expensive, high risk or low-revenue. The larger the company, the more board members from the corporate world were needed to qualify as a serious business entity. Bizarrely, board members from the arts were classed by the funding bodies as 'unskilled', only those from outside the sector were 'skilled'.

Arts funding agencies encouraged this shift towards the corporate model of governance. In 2004 the Australia Council produced a publication recommending that arts boards ideally be composed of members who understood business paradigms.[60] Board members with corporate backgrounds had greater potential to raise money from the private sector—reflecting the US tradition in which sitting on an arts board is conditional on bringing in philanthropic support[61]—and sponsorship from tobacco companies and mining companies was not to be despised. From the corporatist perspective, even if the source of sponsorship did not align with the mission of the organisation, it was not problematic.[62] Artists were expected to be 'grateful' for the largesse that had been bestowed upon them.[63]

Such priorities created serious challenges for arts boards, arts leaders and their companies. Certainly, it could be helpful to have a member on the board who could provide legal advice, but it was often the case that almost every position on the board was taken up by people from outside the arts. How does corporate knowledge contribute when it comes to the problems and processes of making art? What do such board members know about artistic risk, what is 'good' or 'bad' work and how to manage (and value) artistic sensibilities? The boards of organisations in other sectors, whether it be mining, banking, car manufacturing or chocolate making, are composed of experts in their field with an intimate understanding of the sector's professional norms, values and practices. Why not the arts? Why are arts boards dominated by people who know little about the arts? And why is that seen as a good thing by governments? It seems that many, on both sides of politics, believe artists cannot be trusted to govern themselves.

The corporatisation of arts boards, and leadership in the arts generally, has caused considerable harm to the sector.[64] There are egregious examples of boards who have not understood the needs of their organisations, and managers from the corporate world who have shown little support for their artists or understanding of the nature of their institution.[65] The Melbourne Symphony Orchestra 'letting go' its artists while retaining its managers during the pandemic is one example; and the many arts organisations, particularly festivals, who cancelled artists' contracts and offered no compensation, is another.[66]

In 2018 Circus Oz was put 'on fair notice' when it went through a period of reduced earnings.[67] By 2021 it was *not* insolvent but, after a review commissioned by the Australia Council and Creative Victoria, MAPAB recommended that it replace the remaining artists on its board with 'skills based' members: that is, non-arts members. Instead of recognising that the company's revenue was suffering because its mission had been affected by the corporatisation of its board, the MAPAB recommended removing the artists and replacing them with *more* corporate members.[68] Circus Oz was unique in having a core membership of former staff and performers of the circus who elected four of its eleven board members. Corporate delegates were already in the majority, so how could more corporate members succeed in renewing the *artistic vision* of Circus Oz where the existing members had failed? The membership refused to agree to this demand and the board summarily decided to close down the company. When the membership rejected their decision, the board resigned and in early 2022 the membership took back ownership of the company and created a new board.[69]

Isn't it obvious that arts organisations must be driven by arts practice? Knowledge of arts practice has to be at the centre of arts organisations for their governance to be 'fit for purpose'. The values and objectives of the arts are at odds with the corporate sector and generic business paradigms cannot be simply flipped over and applied.

A cultural policy?

The election of Federal Labor under the leadership of Kevin Rudd in 2007 brought new energy to government and raised hopes. The arts had been campaigning for a national cultural policy prior to the election[70] and in April 2008 Rudd convened an 'Australia 2020 Summit' in Canberra to develop national strategies across a range of policy domains.[71] There were ten streams, each with 100 delegates, including 'Creative Australia—the arts, film and design' focused on the arts and culture.

The Summit generated a lot of positive energy, fuelling a belief that Labor would steam ahead to change the broader policy environment, and the National Apology to the Stolen Generations in 2008 seemed to confirm that attitudes in government were changing.[72] There was excitement too when Peter Garrett, a rock musician, was appointed the new minister for the arts, and for a while it seemed that the arts sector was at last rising in the Government's estimation.

But then Garrett was caught up in a scandal in his other portfolio, the environment, a poorly planned national housing insulation program that resulted in the deaths of several young men, Labor became enmeshed in an internal leadership struggle between its right and left factions, and Rudd was replaced by Julia Gillard in an ugly leadership spill in 2010.[73]

Garrett was replaced as minister for the arts by a more experienced politician, Simon Crean. Although interest in the arts was at a low ebb, five years after the Australia Summit he succeeded in persuading his colleagues to support a new national cultural policy. *Creative Australia* was launched in March 2013 and it included recommendations for significant increases in the Australia Council's annual budget allocation, as well as changes to its relationship with the federal government.[74] Once more optimism in the arts community revived. Then Crean called for another spill of the Party leadership. The bid failed and he was sacked and replaced for a short time by Tony Burke, before another spill saw Rudd return to the leadership, but within a few weeks the Labor Party was out of government.[75]

In September 2013 Tony Abbott was elected prime minister of a federal Coalition government and George Brandis became minister for the arts. The urgent funding increases recommended by *Creative Australia* simply disappeared.[76]

Australian artists and arts workers are not generally valued or respected by those in power. They are likely to be critical of the status quo, regardless of who is in office, and Coalition governments align them with the left.[77] When a group of artists boycotted the 2014 Sydney Biennale in protest against its major sponsor, Transfield Holdings, Brandis, as minister for the arts, condemned the action:

> Artists, like everybody else, are entitled to voice their political opinions, but I view with deep concern the effective blackballing of a benefactor, implicit in this decision, merely because of its commercial arrangements.[78]

The Chair of the Biennale Board, Luca Belgiorno-Nettis, was a member of the Belgiorno-Nettis family who owned Transfield Holdings and had been a long-term sponsor of the visual arts in Sydney and the Biennale in particular. Transfield Holdings was a minority shareholder in Transfield Services, a company which had recently taken over the management of the refugee-processing centre on Nauru where Reza Berati had died, from a British security company, G4S.[79] Both Brandis and Malcolm Turnbull (then a senior minister in the Government) released statements scolding the artists for rejecting this source of financial support.[80] Brandis wrote to the Australia Council, demanding that any arts organisation that refused private sector sponsorship be deemed ineligible for public funding.[81]

Perhaps it was this political action by artists that made Brandis decide to take direct control of funding in the arts portfolio. Journalist Miriam Cosic welcomed the change, commenting on *The Drum* that it was a welcome relief to have an 'adult' in charge of the arts.[82] Brandis wanted the power to reward those he considered to be doing 'excellent work' and set up an alternative agency within his own department in order to increase competition or 'contestability' within the sector.[83] In the 2015 budget, the Government went further and announced that the minister would create his own arts fund, the National Programme for Excellence in the Arts (NPEA) and transfer $104.7 million over four years from the Australia Council's budget to support it.[84] The Australia Council's grants to the major performing arts companies, however, were to be protected from funding cuts.

The impact of this raid on the Council's budget fell on the smaller arts organisations and individual artists. Brandis believed that the Council gave preference to certain kinds of artists and no doubt he thought that by removing funds from the peer review system and creating his own agency he was doing the arts a service. But while the arts sector is often divided, it is united on the two principles he had brought under attack: arm's length decision-making and peer review.

Direct political intervention in grant decisions is generally received badly by the arts community and invariably causes significant disruption to the sector. The actions of the minister generated considerable hostility and led to a Senate Inquiry.[85] The Inquiry held public meetings up and down the country and received 2,719 submissions.[86] In December 2015 it produced a report for Parliament that included thirteen recommendations, the first of which was that the development of an arts policy and a planned approach to the equitable distribution of arts funding.[87]

The Brandis experiment did not end well. Malcolm Turnbull replaced Tony Abbott as leader of the Coalition in another leadership spill and Brandis was packed off to England to become the Australian High Commissioner. Mitch Fifield was appointed arts minister in September 2015 and he remained in the portfolio until mid-2019. The NPEA's name was changed to the Catalyst Fund, to give it a more benign appearance, but its original mission as an arts funding program that ran separately from the Australia Council remained intact.

While different funds for different purposes is no bad thing in the arts, removing money from the Council's severely limited annual allocation in order to create a national competitor was disastrous. The Senate Inquiry requested that all the money that had been taken from the Council be restored. A partial restoration of $32 million was made in late 2015 and the Catalyst fund met its demise in 2017.[88] Although the Government under Turnbull promised to return the full amount of $104 million, $23.7 million remains outstanding.

The Australia Council

The upshot of all these interventions was that overall funding for the Australia Council in 2021 was less than it had been under the Labor Government in 2013.[89] The Council had fallen into a trap in 2014, when it had tried to manage its reduced funding allocation by guaranteeing longer-term funding for a smaller number of applicants. When Brandis withdrew millions from its budget the following year to fund his own agency, the Council was faced with the problem of how to fund these commitments. It changed its decision-making process and, with the exception of the First Nations Arts and Culture Board, replaced the art form boards with ad hoc peer assessment panels to be convened as needed.

The reaction of the arts sector was first shock and then silence. The art form boards had been a constant of the Council since its inception and there was much disquiet. The essential characteristic of the older model had been the overview it gave of the sectors as a whole, but the 'peer pool' that replaced the boards had no role in making policy. The opportunity to explore and assert the social purpose of cultural practice was disappearing under long lists of KPIs.

From 2013–16 funding for individual artists sank by 70%.[90] After 2016 there was a dramatic reduction in Council support for arts companies across the country. By 2020, a total of 96 companies had been cut from its client base.[91] These actions have alienated the Council from its core constituency, the arts sector itself. Over the past twenty years the Council has become less engaged with the arts community, less transparent and more bureaucratic.

The Council lost leadership when it failed to publicly oppose the actions of Brandis in 2015. In the eyes of the arts community it had become over-compliant and was leaving the sector itself to fight for the restoration of its annual budget allocation. Since then, many more troubling decisions have been made at the Council that have led to diverse programs in youth arts, community arts and new technology initiatives being terminated. There has been little consultation with the sector and the Federal Government has continued to distance itself from the Council while, at the same time, its ministers intervene to decide arts grants and ignore the processes that were designed to ensure the fair and equitable distribution of funds.

Ministerial patronage and government rorting of arts grants

Government intervention in arts subsidy has increased dramatically in the past decade. Further, there has been abuse of the funding system and interference in grant decisions, peer recommendations have been ignored to suit political preferences, and funds have been allotted to marginal seats and party supporters. Several arts organisations in marginal electorates were given large grants from the Catalyst Fund in 2016–18.[92] The same happened in various community grants programs.[93] The rorting of government grants is not something that can be dismissed lightly.

In New South Wales, the minister for the arts, Don Harwin, took a 'hands on' approach to arts grants on several occasions. In 2018 he admitted that he had re-directed funding that had been allocated to eleven arts organisations by the ministerial arts advisory committee to the Sydney Symphony Orchestra;[94] and in 2019 to allocating regional arts grants to organisations based on their political affiliations. Thirteen of the projects he funded were considered lacking in merit by his own regional arts funding committee.[95] In early 2021 it was revealed that only $13 million of a fund of $50 million, set up by the NSW Government in 2020 to support arts organisations and artists affected by Covid closures, had been given out. Of this, just under half, $6 million, had been allocated to *one* organisation, the Sydney Theatre Company—again at the direction of the minister.[96] In late 2020 the then NSW premier, Gladys Berejiklian, admitted that $140 million in government grants had been allocated to mostly safe Coalition seats prior to the State election, and while she agreed that this could be seen as 'pork barrelling', she argued, it was not an illegal practice.[97] In early 2022, the NSW auditor general, Margaret Crawford, described the practice of pork barrelling as 'lacking integrity' in a report to the NSW State Parliament, when noting that 96% of the grants in the Stronger Communities Fund, worth $250 million, had been awarded to safe Coalition seats in NSW with little evidence to support the decision.[98] In 2021 Prime Minister Scott Morrison admitted that four times as many government grants had been awarded to Coalition than Labor seats, but, he declared, this was merely a reflection of good local members.[99]

Normalising unethical behaviour damages Australia's democracy. It has certainly warped advocacy in the arts. Fear of government retribution has become commonplace and artists and arts organisations are now loath to publicly criticise funding bodies, even when the decisions they make are demonstrably flawed. Instead they lobby ministers personally to influence their decisions. The distribution of taxpayer's money should be treated as a matter of utmost probity, but the scrutiny arts organisations are put under is galling when the ministers themselves apparently regard the ethical use of taxpayer's money as irrelevant.

Onward and downward

In the years after 2016 the downward trajectory continued. Another leadership spill saw Scott Morrison replace Malcolm Turnbull as prime minister in August 2018. Paul Fletcher became minister for the arts following the re-election of the Coalition in 2019 and Mitch Fifield left domestic politics to become Australia's representative to the United Nations.

Morrison showed little interest in the arts and merged the Office of the Arts with the Department of Infrastructure, Transport, Regional Development and Communication, eliminating the Arts from the title of the new department all together. Back in 1972 Gough Whitlam had celebrated the centrality of the arts to the nation's identity by appointing himself arts minister, but by the start of 2020, the Coalition Government had rendered the arts politically invisible.

The arts community protested their treatment at the onset of the pandemic and, perhaps prompted by this, a Parliamentary Inquiry was announced in August 2020 to investigate the significant impact Covid was having on the industry, as well as the benefits the arts brought to Australia.[100] It was convened by the House of Representatives Standing Committee on Communications and the Arts. The Inquiry included in its methodology an online survey, written submissions and it invited certain individuals and organisations to address the Committee directly. The terms of reference were muddled and overly broad and there was confusion from the outset, but despite this it received 4,871 responses to the survey and 352 submissions. The Committee's report to Parliament on 28 October 2021 contained 21 recommendations and asked for a progress report from the minister by December 2022.[101] *Again it recommended,* like the 2015 Senate Inquiry before, that the Government develop a national cultural plan to address the short- and long-term needs of the sector. It also recommended that the term 'arts' be restored to the title of its government department. The challenge then, as in 2015, was how to get the Coalition government to take on board *any* of these recommendations, however bland, and move forward with them.

As the pandemic progressed, the Government showed little understanding of the complexity of the arts and cultural sector, downplaying the role of the Australia Council in arts policy and funding decisions at the same time as it tried to dominate the cultural agenda through its main model of arts and cultural support, the RISE fund. RISE was controlled by the federal minister with advice from non-specialists in his department and large amounts of money were given to applicants with no reference to the quality or significance of their work. Funds were skewed towards activities that proposed to employ large numbers or attract large audiences, even if the figures were rather fanciful. There was also a preference for commercial activities. Given how little money has been made available to the arts over the past decade, it was hard to witness large amounts of so-called arts money going to companies like Lego and TedX while artists themselves were struggling to survive.

Artists must be involved in the decisions and recommendations on arts grants. When the arts become a political tool, the integrity of its practices and the protection of cultural heritage both suffer. It is time all political parties stepped back and let artists make their own decisions. If the arts were able to take risks and make decisions, free from intimidation and political influence, the outcome would be better for everyone.

***

Since *Creative Nation* in 1994, neither major political party has demonstrated a meaningful commitment to the arts at the federal level. *Creative Australia* in 2013 was a short-lived policy that did not deliver any major benefits and in nine years of Coalition government, the sector experienced only turmoil and neglect, that reached its pinnacle in the pandemic. The arms' length principle continued to be eroded; the amount of Australian content in film and television was reduced; engagement with other countries through the showcasing of Australian arts abroad flagged; and artistic collaboration with other countries via cultural exchanges fell off. Since 2007, federal arts funding has declined as a proportion of the nation's GDP by 18.9%.[102] Canada, by contrast, a country not unlike Australia, has managed to *increase* its arts and cultural budget by $1.9 billion.[103]

Corporatisation and economisation of arts policy has changed the way the arts are valued, framed, and managed. This in turn has affected the leadership of arts organisations and promoted relationships with government that are fixated on economics. These changes, that convert arts organisations into commercial enterprises, have devalued artists and arts practice. Their reductive paradigm, that focuses on the bottom line rather than the complex nature of arts practice and the unique benefits it brings to society, has not served the best interests of the arts or Australia. Without realising it, the whole concept of what we know as the 'arts', has shifted. What we urgently need now is to resist the urge to rush on to the new and rediscover what is essential by going back to the basics.

Australia's Unique Resource

The pandemic was a wake-up call. Now, more than ever, the arts have become a part of our daily lives, no longer something only 'the elite' enjoy but an expression of an interconnected system of collective wellbeing. It is vital to ensure that arts practices continue to grow across our entire community, and that everyone has access to them. The arts reflect our whole culture, and our cultures are what make us who we are. When our culture is at the heart of our collective life, appropriate funding and support should naturally follow.

To escape the reductive concepts that we have normalized, we need to think about what we understand by 'the arts', and what they mean to us. What do we understand by 'culture' and how does it manifest in our lives? If we start by asking these questions, we can make sense of the debate and find a way forward that works in our own unique cultural, social and political context.

While government funding for the arts has been eroding over the past fifty years, public respect for Aboriginal and Torres Strait Islander arts and culture has grown. Art centres like Papunya Tjupi Arts, Maningrida and Warlukurlangu and artists such as Emily Kame Kngwarreye, Rover Thomas and Gloria, Doreen and Jeannie Petyarre; the music of Geoffrey Gurrumul Yunupingu and Yothi Yindi; and the acting, dancing and storytelling of David Gulpilil Ridjimiraril Dalaithngu; dance and theatre companies such as Bangarra and Black Theatre, Ilbijerri, and Kooemba Jdarra and performers such as Deborah Mailman, Rachael Maza, Rachel Perkins, Christine Anu, Deborah Cheetham, Stephen Page, Ernie Dingo, Archie Roach, Wesley Enoch and Warwick Thornton, have come to represent the very best in contemporary Australian arts practice. Their impact on the wider Australian culture has been profound. They have changed our national culture—and ourselves—and enriched us with their creative work.

First Nations art is also a valuable export industry, but traditional arts and cultural practices, as well as languages, are being lost every day, and despite their outstanding contribution and international status, many First Nations artists live and work in intolerable conditions. The destruction of Juukun Gorge shocked the world and no amount of profit can compensate. As a nation, we need to make a profound adjustment, and begin to recognise that our First Nations are a unique cultural *resource* and follow their example by showing respect for our artists, our culture, our institutions, our elders and our environment.

The state has a legitimate role to play in managing the extremes of capitalism by *regulating* market forces to protect the common good. During the pandemic it has intervened to prevent businesses from profiting from the crisis. The same imperative compels the state to protect our cultural heritage from destruction and foster the arts. Cultural institutions such as libraries, museums and galleries play a pivotal role in communities and we would be bereft without them. They need to be able to digitise collections, provide adequate storage facilities and display and offer public access to the wonderful treasures they contain. It is a shocking indictment that the National Archives had to resort to 'crowdfunding' in order to digitise rapidly deteriorating collections in 2021.[104] Cultural heritage should be preserved and protected from destruction by manmade or natural causes. Australia is a signatory to the United Nations Educational, Scientific and Cultural Organization's (UNESCO) declarations on culture, cultural diversity and arts practices.[105] We are obliged to honour them by ensuring that our museums, galleries, archives and libraries are adequately resourced.

The threats to our culture are not just physical. Monopolisation of our commercial networks and media has seen Australian stories pushed off our screens by international product. The

Murdoch family controls 70% of print media in Australia and has controlling interests in Foxtel and Sky News.[106] Such dominance gives media conglomerates enormous political influence and disproportionate control over the dissemination of public information. In this environment our public broadcasters, the ABC, SBS and NITV, play a crucial role in creating, reflecting and critiquing Australian culture. However, during the pandemic, rather than supporting the arts sector, the Federal Government suspended local content quotas for commercial broadcasters as part of its 'support' package.[107] From 2014 to 2020 the ABC lost $783 million in government funding[108] at the same time as the public media agencies were subjected to attacks on their integrity.[109] All this has meant that work opportunities for Australian filmmakers, writers, actors, designers and musicians will decrease, but the failure to protect our public broadcasters and maintain Australian content on our screens represents more than job losses, it threatens the infrastructure of our national culture.

***

There is abundant evidence to show that the government's financial support for the arts and culture has significantly reduced over the years. Until the recent change of government, the arts didn't even rate a mention in the title of their own department. Even worse, grants were being routinely awarded to communities in marginal electorates for party political purposes. Yet we know that the arts are a public good and that Australia is a wealthy country that can afford to provide adequate funding. So what needs to change?

For the past twenty years arts advocates have asked for a national cultural policy or a national arts plan. This has been reinforced by recommendations from two parliamentary committees within the past seven years. Yet, aside from Labor's short-lived national cultural policy, *Creative Australia*, there has been no attempt, at a national level, since 1994 to address the needs of the sector or create a comprehensive plan for the future. In May 2022 a Labor federal government was elected. Minister for the Arts, Tony Burke, announced the development of a new national cultural policy based on *Creative Australia* to be published by the end of 2022.[110] Although the process and time that was allowed for consultation was less than ideal, this is positive news. Relying on the political goodwill of governments to bring about change has not proved effective in the past and it remains to be seen, in the light of the major challenges ahead, if this new policy will be fit for purpose.

Bipartisanship is rare in politics and policy developed by one side of government can be quickly undone when the opposition comes to power. Many countries resolve this problem with a ministry of culture. An Australian ministry of culture might include in its ambit the arts, First Nations arts and heritage, public broadcasting, film, and cultural heritage. All these areas are interconnected through their association with 'culture', and placing them together in an integrated and central location would help bring them into the political mainstream.

While there might be concerns that a ministry of culture could extend government control over arts practice, this could be prevented by use of the arm's length principle of funding and peer review. Political intervention in grant decisions is in no-one's interest and reduces the credibility of the government and its ministers. All major cultural organisations could then be funded directly by the government from within this department as part of a national cultural heritage framework.

The list would include our major galleries, libraries, museums, archives and other national entities that are already direct-line funded, such as Screen Australia and the Australia Council. It could also include the major performing arts organisations, as they also represent aspects of our cultural heritage. That is, the State orchestras, the national opera company and perhaps a national theatre company. Having a ministry responsible for everything within the ambit of culture would ensure that national protocols were put in place to protect the national interest against the commercial interests of private enterprise.

All public broadcasting would be part of this ministry to prevent commercial interests from dominating the discourse. Entities such as the ABC, SBS and NITV enjoy public trust and are critical to the national debate, freedom of expression and the right of citizens to hold politicians and their governments to account. They play a significant role in presenting Australian stories on our screens and commissioning work from Australian writers, filmmakers and performers. SBS has challenged the homogenous norms of Australian culture and ethnicity and ensured the inclusion of a range of voices in the public sphere. NITV has provided a voice for our First Nations people and raised awareness and understanding of the culture within the wider population.

Middle-size and smaller arts organisations and individual artists would continue to be funded by the Australia Council; and film would continue to be funded through Screen Australia. It might also be helpful to establish a new statutory authority, similar to the Australian Foundation for Culture and Humanities that was lost in a change of government thirty years ago. This entity could address the gap between community cultural heritage, local history and community arts, and ensure that grants were awarded at arm's length from political interests.

Establishing these entities and creating a formal ministerial structure that provided a central home for all these activities and functions would acknowledge the importance of culture, heritage and the arts in all our lives. Obviously, this entity would not be a cure-all, but it would allow for the development of a critical mass of shared interests and knowledge that, over time, would benefit the whole country; and placing cultural entities, arts, heritage and communication agencies into the one central location would make them more powerful as a group.

It is to be hoped that the forthcoming national cultural policy will provide a considered plan for the development of arts and culture, that allows goals to be set and ensures that the decisions made by government are proactive. The pandemic experience has demonstrated that if we do not develop clear policies, then the sectors that are currently excluded from the political framework, such as the arts, could be sent to the wall. Australia needs to mature as a nation by taking its arts and culture seriously, and a Ministry of Culture would provide a platform for the nation's identity.

We must all take responsibility for caring for our country and our culture. This means placing the arts at the centre of our thinking. We can do this—and we need to do this—to ensure our nation has a positive and creative future. We are a wealthy country both materially and culturally. We need to acknowledge this and act upon it, so that all future generations can enjoy their culture and practise their arts. As our First Nations' people have told us, arts, culture and country are all one.

Endnotes

1. Australian Institute of Aboriginal and Torres Strait Islander Studies (AIATSIS), 'Art and Authenticity'. *AIATSIS*. May 25, 2022. https://aiatsis.gov.au/. .
2. Deanna Kemp, John Owen and Rodger Barnes, 'Juukan Gorge inquiry puts Rio Tinto on notice, but without drastic reforms, it could happen again'. *The Conversation*. December 9, 2020. http://theconversation.com.
3. Greg Jericho, 'The Morrison government is trying to lock in a less equitable economy for years to come'. *The Guardian*. August 15, 2020. https://www.theguardian.com.
4. Ben Eltham and Alison Pennington, 'Creativity in Crisis: Rebooting Australia's arts and entertainment sector after COVID'. *Australia Institute*. July 26, 2021. www.australiainstitute.org.au,
5. Bureau of Communications and Arts Research, *Cultural and Creative Activity in Australia 2008-09 to 2016-17*. Department of Communication and the Arts (Australia), Working Paper, October, 2018. https://apo.org.au.
6. *I Lost My Gig*. https://ilostmygig.net.au/
7. David Throsby and Katya Petetskaya, *Making Art Work: an economic study of professional artists in Australia*. Australia Council for the Arts. September, 2017. *Australia Council for the Arts*. www.australiacouncil.gov.au
8. Nathan Cooper, '$27 million for arts organisations in new targeted support package'. *Sydney Morning Herald*. April 9, 2020. www.smh.com.au.
9. JobKeeper was a wage subsidy of $1,500 per fortnight to keep people in jobs, and paid to the employer, if the employee had been in employment with that employer for more than twelve months. JobSeeker was an allowance of around $1,100 for those made unemployed by the pandemic.
10. Paul Fletcher, 'Coronavirus hit Australia's arts industry hard and early. Our support package is designed to help.' *The Guardian*. April 23, 2020. https://www.theguardian.com.

11. Matthew Doran, 'Coronavirus JobKeeper package passes Parliament after Labor amendments fail'. *ABC News*. April 8, 2020. www.abc.net.au.
12. Gina Fairley, 'MEAA supports musicians in Opera Australia stand down'. *ArtsHub*. March 19, 2020. www.artshub.com.au.
13. Linda Morris, 'Opera Australia offers lifeline to stood-down staff'. *Sydney Morning Herald*. March 16, 2020. www.smh.com.au.
14. Nick Miller, 'Struggling Melbourne Symphony Orchestra "stands down" all musicians'. *The Age*. April 14, 2020. www.theage.com.au.
15. Nick Miller, 'Musicians say breakdown with MSO management "irreparable"'. *The Age*. May 29, 2020. www.theage.com.au.
16. Ben Eltham and Alison Pennington, op. cit.
17. Jordan Hayne and Dan Conifer, 'Government to hand out $25k grants for housing construction, renovations to bolster industry'. *ABC News*. June 3, 2020. www.abc.net.au; 'New analysis: arts & entertainment funding creates 10x more jobs for women than HomeBuilder'. Media Release. *Australia Institute*. May 13, 2021. www.australiainstitute.org.au.
18. Naomi Moy and Francesco Paolucci, 'Restructuring higher education funding in Australia during a pandemic'. *Independent Australia*. July 9, 2020. https://independentaustralia.net.
19. 'Business Indicators, Business Impacts of Covid-19'. *Australian Bureau of Statistics*. Week commencing March 30, 2020. www.abs.gov.au.
20. Brendan Coates, Matthew Cowgill, Tony Chen, Will Mackey, 'The charts that show coronavirus pushing up to a quarter of the workforce out of work'. *The Conversation*. April 19, 2020. www.theconversation.com.
21. Jo Caust, 'No minister, creative arts are not a "lifestyle choice"'. *InDaily*. October 24, 2016. https://indaily.com.au.
22. Eltham and Pennington op. cit.
23. Office for the Arts. *Restart Investment to Sustain and Expand (RISE) Fund*. https://www.arts.gov.au/funding-and-support/rise-fund.

24. 'Forecast Opportunity View—RISE2020'. *GrantConnect*. www.grants.gov.au.

25. Joanna Mendelssohn, 'Getting with the program: Brandis releases his draft arts funding guidelines'. *The Conversation*. July 2, 2015. www.theconversation.com.

26. Matthew Knott, 'Turnbull government overhauls George Brandis' arts "slush fund"'. *Sydney Morning Herald*. November 19, 2015. www.smh.com.au.

27. Ben Eltham, 'Australia's cultural sector is haemorrhaging money, but the Federal Government isn't interested in stemming the flow'. *The Guardian*. May 26, 2020. https://www.theguardian.com.

28. 'National, State and Territory Population'. *Australian Bureau of Statistics*. March, 2021. www.abs.gov.au.

29. *Creating Our Future: results of the National Arts Participation Survey*. Australia Council for the Arts. August, 2020. *Australia Council for the Arts*. www.australiacouncil.gov.au.

30. *The Big Picture: Public Expenditure on Artistic, Cultural and Creative Activity in Australia*. A New Approach, Australian Academy of the Humanities, Insight Research Series, Report One, 2019. *Australian Academy of the Humanities*. www.humanities.org.au.

31. Ibid.

32. 'The right to freedom of artistic expression and creation (2013)'. *United Nations Human Rights, Office of the High Commissioner*. www.ohchr.org

33. 'Ten Common Questions about a Human Rights Act for Australia'. *Australian Human Rights Commission*. www.humanrights.gov.au.

34. Anthony Shorrocks, James Davies and Rodrigo Lluberas, *Global Wealth Report 2021*. Credit Suisse Research Institute. *Credit Suisse*. www.credit-suisse.com.

35. Peter Davidson, Peter Saunders, Bruce Bradbury and Melissa Wong,

Poverty in Australia 2020—Part 1: Overview. Australian Council of Social Service, University of New South Wales. February 21, 2020. *Australian Policy and Observatory*. https://apo.org.au.

36. Ibid.
37. Daniel Ziffer, 'Basic income is considered a radical idea. But in 2020 we lived it and some people want it back'. *ABC News*. December 9, 2021. www.abc.net.au.
38. Kate Raworth, *Doughnut Economics: Seven Ways to Think Like a 21st-Century Economist*. Random House, 2017.
39. 'Australian fossil fuel subsidies hit $10.3 billion in 2020-21'. Media Release. *Australia Institute*. April 26, 2021. www.australiainstitute.org.au.
40. Daivd Throsby and Katya Petetskaya, op. cit.
41. John Gardiner-Garden, 'Arts Policy in Australia: a history of commonwealth involvement in the arts', Parliamentary Research Service, Background Paper, no. 5, 1994. *Parliament of Australia*. www.aph.gov.au.
42. Paul Boyce, 'Public Goods Definition'. *BoyceWire*. March 23, 2021. www.boycewire.com.
43. Anna Upchurch, *The Origins of the Arts Council Movement: Philanthropy and policy*. Palgrave MacMillan, 2016.
44. Gough Whitlam, *The Whitlam Government 1972-1975*. Viking, 1985, p. 553.
45. John Gardiner-Garden op. cit.
46. Ben Eltham, *When the Goalposts Move*. Platform Papers, no. 48. Currency House, 2016.
47. Jennifer Craik, *Re-visioning Arts and Cultural Policy: Current impasses and future directions*, 'Appendix G.2. Industries Assistance Commission. 1976. Assistance to the Performing Arts. Canberra: AGPS'. ANU Press, 2007. http://doi.org/10.22459/RACP.07.2007.
48. Timothy Pascoe quoted in John Gardiner-Garden, 'Commonwealth Arts Policy and Administration'. Department of Parliamentary Services, Social

Policy Section, Background Note, May 7, 2009. *Parliament of Australia.* www.aph.gov.au.

49. Julian Meyrick, 'No (is a one word poem)'. *The Conversation.* May 25, 2016. www.theconversation.com.
50. Alison Croggon, 'The desertification of Australian culture'. *The Monthly.* October 2019. www.themonthly.com.au.
51. J. W. Nevile, 'Economic Rationalism: social philosophy masquerading as economic science'. The Australia Institute, Background Paper No. 7, May 1997, p.9.
52. John Gardiner-Garden (1994) op. cit.
53. Donald Horne, *The Public Culture: the triumph of industrialism.* Pluto Press, 1986.
54. Paul Keating, Election Speech, Melbourne February 14, 1996. *Australian Federal Election Speeches.* https://electionspeeches.moadoph.gov.au/
55. 'Discussion Paper: Cultural and Creative Activity Satellite Accounts, Australia, 2013', 'Section 3: Defining Cultural and Creative Activity'. National Centre for Culture and Recreation Statistics. June 2013. *Australian Bureau of Statistics.* www.abs.gov.au.
56. 'About Us'. *Creative Partnerships Australia.* https://creativepartnerships.gov.au.
57. 'The Nugent Inquiry into the Major Performing Arts'. Completed Inquiries 1999-02. *Parliament of Australia.* www.aph.gov.au.
58. *National Opera Review,* Final Report, Department of Communications and the Arts, Commonwealth of Australia, 2016. *Office of the Arts.* www.arts.gov.au.
59. Rosemary Neill, 'Play School', *The Australian,* Weekend Review, June 17-18, 2006.
60. Australia Council, *Principles of Corporate Governance and Good Practice Recommendations for the Major Performing Arts Sector.* Major Performing Arts Board, 2004.

61. Francie Ostrower, *Trustees of Culture: Power, Wealth, and Status on Elite Arts Boards*. Chicago University Press, 2002.
62. Alex Kelly, 'The arts in Australia need to break up with fossil fuels'. *Overland*. September 30, 2021. www.overland.org.au.
63. Richard Watts, 'When to say no to sponsorship'. *ArtsHub*. December 9, 2019. www.artshub.com.au.
64. Joanna Trilling and Rebecca Trigger, 'Dumping of Black Swan executive director Natalie Jenkins criticised by Janet Holmes a Court'. *ABC News*. May 29, 2019. www.abc.net.au.
65. Judith White, *Culture Heist: Art Versus Money*. Brandl & Schlesinger, 2017.
66. Kelly Burke, '"Absolutely heartbroken": event cancellations return to devastate Australia's music industry'. *The Guardian*. December 21, 2021. https://www.theguardian.com.
67. Elissa Blake, 'What went wrong at Circus Oz? The story behind the veteran company's "devastating" downfall'. *The Guardian*. December 11, 2021. https://www.theguardian.com.
68. Tully Barnett, Julian Meyrick and Justin O'Connor, 'Circus Oz: a crisis in a crisis'. *ArtsHub*. December 22, 2021. www.artshub.com.au.
69. Richard Watts, 'The rebuilding of Circus Oz begins'. *ArtsHub*. February 18, 2022. www.artshub.com.au.
70. David Throsby, *Does Australia Need a Cultural Policy?* Platform Papers No. 7. Currency House, January 2006.
71. *Australia 2020 Summit*, Final Report. Department of Prime Minister and Cabinet, Commonwealth of Australia, May 2020. *Australian Policy and Observatory*. https://apo.org.au.
72. Kevin Rudd, 'National Apology to the Stolen Generations', 2008. *National Museum Australia*. www.nma.gov.au.
73. Jean Parker, 'Lessons to be learnt from the pink batts disaster'. *The Drum*. May 21, 2014. www.abc.net.au.

74. Simon Crean, *Creative Australia National Cultural Policy. Parliament of Australia*, 2013. *Parliament of Australia*. www.aph.gov.au.
75. 'Crean sacked as minister'. *Sydney Morning Herald*. March 21, 2013. www.smh.com.au.
76. Ben Eltham, 'Arts cuts: Abbott Government takes us backwards'. *ArtsHub*. May 14, 2014. www.artshub.com.au.
77. George Megalogenis, 'And now for something completely different'. *The Monthly*. December 2020–January 2021, pp. 10-13.
78. Bridie Jabour, 'George Brandis threatens Sydney Biennale over Transfield "blackballing"'. *The Guardian*. March 13, 2014. https://www.theguardian.com.
79. Peter Tregear, 'Biennale and Brandis: when art and politics collide'. *ABC News*. March 14, 2014. www.abc.net.au.
80. Bridie Jabour, 'Malcolm Turnbull slams Biennale's "vicious ingratitude" to Transfield'. *The Guardian*. March 11, 2014. https://www.theguardian.com; Sarah Joseph, 'The Biennale Boycott Blues'. *The Conversation*. March 22, 2014. www.theconversation.com.
81. Roger Benjamin, 'We should value the Biennale protest, not threaten arts funding'. *The Conversation*. March 13, 2014. www.theconversation.com.
82. Miriam Cosic, 'An adult is back in charge of the arts'. *ABC News*. September 25, 2013. www.abc.net.au.
83. George Brandis quoted in Martin McKenzie-Murray, 'Inside George Brandis's Australia Council arts heist'. *The Saturday Paper*. May 23, 2015. www.thesaturdaypaper.com.au.
84. Ben Eltham, 'Budget 2015: George Brandis' extraordinary raid of the Australia Council'. *ABC News*. May 13, 2015. www.abc.net.au.
85. The Senate, Legal and Constitutional Affairs, References Committee, 'Impact of the 2014 and 2015 Commonwealth Budget Decisions on the Arts'. Parliament House, Canberra, December 2015. *Parliament of Australia*. www.aph.gov.au.

86. Ibid.

87. Ibid.

88. 'BREAKING: Catalyst scrapped after almost two years of arts funding chaos'. *Daily Review*. March 18, 2017. www.dailyreview.com.au.

89. Gabrielle Trainor and Angus James, 'Review of the Australia Council'. Commonwealth Government, Canberra, May 2012. *Australian Policy and Observatory*. https://apo.org.au.

90. Alison Croggon, 'The 70% drop in Australia Council grants for individual artists is staggering'. *The Guardian*. May 19, 2016. https://www.theguardian.com.

91. Ben Eltham, 'We are witnessing a cultural bloodbath in Australia that has been years in the making'. *The Guardian*. April 6, 2020. https://www.theguardian.com.

92. 'Sir Hans Heysen's Adelaide Hills home The Cedars could become "MONA of South Australia"'. *ABC News*. April 22, 2016. www.abc.net.au.

93. David Crowe, 'Morrison government's grants analysis reveals a system for taxpayers that must change'. *Sydney Morning Herald*. December 15, 2021. www.smh.com.au.

94. Michaela Boland and Penny Timms, 'Arts Minister admits funds redirected to Sydney Symphony Orchestra'. *ABC News*. September 26, 2018. www.abc.net.au.

95. Michaela Boland and Greg Miskelly, 'NSW Deputy Premier John Barilaro, Don Harwin accused of "pork-barrelling" in Coalition seats before State election'. *ABC News*. May 25, 2020. www.abc.net.au.

96. Kelly Burke, '"Ridiculous" secrecy: confusion surrounds fate of $7m arts bailout money in $50m NSW government scheme'. *The Guardian*. January 14, 2021. https://www.theguardian.com.

97. Finbar O'Mallon, 'NSW Premier Gladys Berejiklian says controversial grants program was pork barrelling'. *Australian Financial Review*. November 26, 2020. www.afr.com.

98. NSW auditor-general publishes damning report into government grant scheme at centre of pork-barrelling claims'. *ABC News*. February 8, 2022. www.abc.net.au.
99. David Crowe, 'Morrison government's grants analysis reveals a system for taxpayers that must change'. *Sydney Morning Herald*. December 15, 2021. www.smh.com.au.
100. 'State of the Arts in 2020 and Beyond: new inquiry'. Media Release. *Parliament of Australia*. August 27, 2020. www.aph.gov.au.
101. 'Sparking the Arts Sector'. Media Release. *Parliament of Australia*. October 27, 2021. www.aph.gov.au; House of Representatives Standing Committee on Communications and the Arts, 'Sculpting a National Cultural Plan: Igniting a post-COVID economy for the arts', 'List of Recommendations'. *Parliament of Australia*. October 2021. www.aph.gov.au.
102. Elissa Blake, 'Australia's arts sector shredded by latest Covid shutdown and won't survive without government help, report warns'. *The Guardian*. July 26, 2021. https://www.theguardian.com.
103. 'Growing the Middle Class', Government of Canada, Federal Budget, 2016. *Government of Canada*. www.open.canada.ca
104. Katina Curtis and Shane Wright, 'Archive passes the hat in desperate bid to save Australia's history'. *Sydney Morning Herald*. May 16, 2021. www.smh.com.au.
105. UNESCO, 'Convention for the Safeguarding of the Intangible Cultural Heritage', October 17, 2003. Document code: MISC/2003/CLT/CH/14. *Convention on the Protection and Promotion of the Diversity of Cultural Expressions*. October 20, 2005. Document code: CLT.2005/CONVENTION DIVERSITE-CULT REV.2. www. unesco.org.
106. Lavender Baj, 'Here's exactly how far Rupert Murdoch's media empire stretches in Australia and beyond'. *Pedestrian*. November 11, 2020. www.pedestrian.tv.

107. Paul Karp, 'Local content quotas suspended in $54m package for Australia's coronavirus-hit media'. *The Guardian*. April 15, 2020. https://www.theguardian.com.

108. Amanda Meade, 'ABC loses $783m funding since 2014 when Coalition made its first cuts'. *The Guardian*. May 4, 2020. https://www.theguardian.com.

109. Vincent O'Donnell, 'Is the ABC really biased?' *Sydney Morning Herald*. June 30, 2018. www.smh.com.au.

110. 'A new era for Australia'. Media Release. *Minister for the Arts*. July 1, 2022. https://minister.infrastructure.gov.au/burke/media-release,

The Trouble with this Canoe

Tyson Yunkaporta

I'm having trouble with this canoe I've made. I didn't know it was 'art' until somebody exhibited it, and at that moment it became capital in which investors might park their wealth. It is an ocean-going canoe, from a time when international trade between us and the lands to the north of our continent was different.

Ours was a *give-and-give* economy, not *give-and-take*, as those who believe in ancient free market instincts of reciprocity like to tell us. There was no invisible hand entity guiding us, only the Law of the land. In embassy and trade, we shared this *give-and-give* relation across the sea to the north. This relation enriched us, not with growth, but with increase. Our increase-based economy measured wealth in the multiplication of connections rather than the hoarding of resources and credit.

I'm having trouble with this canoe, because it exists now in a skewed *give-and-take* economy. It is art now, because there are layers of abstraction and extraction between the canoe and the ocean of life it is supposed to travel. Works like these have always been expressions of spirit and relation so profoundly grounded in Country that we have never had abstract nouns to describe them as an asset class before. But it is dispossessed now by the word 'art'.

However, Australia's First Peoples are not befuddled victims of abstractions arising from the financial system that spawned the arts, because we were there when it all began, and we were part of its conception and development.

My family was there five centuries ago, BC (before capital) when a sailing ship landed at *Keer Weer*, which (spoiler alert) is Dutch for 'turn back'. The Apalech Clan has a totemic relation with brolga, an Australian species of crane, and the Dutch had a similar relation at the time through a folk-totemic triad of crane, goose and stork. Those three birds had a sacred role in the birthing and nurturing of children. In the old days, the Dutch could always tell how many children lived in a house by the number of stork nests on the roof.

This would later be dismissed as superstition, when it was noted that storks build their nests on chimneys and the number of children one had depended on how many fireplaces one could afford to install, in order to heat a living space for them. It became a cautionary tale for statisticians warning about the folly of mistaking correlation for causation.

However, half a millennium ago, the crane worked with the goose and the stork in the sacred role of bringing the spirit into new-born infants, dancing with people the same way our brolga dances with us. This dance was not art or performance—it was ceremony that could not be separated from life and increase.

The Dutch landing on Western Cape York in the far north of Australia did not establish relations through crane story and dance though, because they were in debt and needed to extract riches to pay for their journey. They gave our clan goods that were unwanted and expected to take something in return. Unfortunately, they tried to take the women. They thought this was reasonable because women were chattel in their culture, but our aunties didn't see it the same way and so there was trouble. If the Dutchmen had asked a girl to dance first, maybe our global financial system would look very different today, along with the artistic disciplines that always arise from human economic relations with the land.

I'm having trouble with this canoe. It is a ghost canoe rendered as art by way of history and economics. I'm sure they knew the same trouble in Europe half a millennium ago.

In Europe at the time, art was still integrated with life and land for the peasantry, but it had become separate from reality in the upper classes through a system of patronage. If you wanted to produce an opera you had to rely on funding from some bloated prince who might tell you there could be no dancing in the performance because it was sinful. He may also have forced you to spend half your time tutoring his tone-deaf niece on the harpsichord. The same pattern existed for ocean-going traders, who would be funded by the merchant class and captained by the incompetent friends and family members of oligarchs, for voyages that were expected to produce exotic goods and people to sell, or else the trader would face debtor's prison.

We can only imagine the economic pressures weighing on those sailors from Holland, the stresses that would drive them to ignore their folkloric foundation and fail to make proper embassy in their trading relations at Keer Weer. For whatever reason, there was no brolga/crane ceremonial exchange of story, image and dance, and the ladies were not interested in becoming chattel, so spears were thrown.

It went badly for the Dutchmen, most of whom died on that beach, leaving a skeleton crew to limp home with nothing to show for their voyage. Debtor's prison was not a pleasant experience, so not long after that they sought to find a mechanism, a loophole for avoiding financial accountability, and the world's first corporation was born. In short order, they invented the modern financial market as we know it, along with arts speculation. So, if you're looking for somebody to blame for NFTs, look no further than the Dutch. Although, a case could be made that our clan's harsh response to artless trade protocols was the catalyst. The spear shot heard around the world!

The speculative world of finance has always been risky though, even with a corporation in place as a fake but legally sentient 'person' to absorb financial accountability for losses. Kingdoms rise and fall and there are wars that can kill off up to a quarter of your population when you are tinkering with an economic structure that has the capacity to hardwire inequity into the system permanently. Old money in Europe has always known how to survive the apocalypses that come with such a project—store your surplus wealth in long-term capital that can endure world wars and the death of nations. Your portfolio must contain investments in three resilient classes of assets—land, precious metals and art.

The only catch is that these assets only retain and accumulate value over time according to their limitability and excludability, so you need to maintain a controlling stake in current and emergent political systems, ensuring that access to land and culture is limited and that increasing numbers of people are excluded each year. Demand must exceed supply, or wealth cannot grow.

Diabolical layers of abstraction must be installed to remove people and limit their access to land and culture. Land becomes an abstraction known as real estate and land-based culture becomes an abstraction known as art. You can only access these things in accordance with your level of economic privilege. The more limited the access, the more value accrues.

Land became real estate through a technology known as mortgage, which was originally designed as a legal mechanism to assist in the enclosure of the commons and the removal of land-based communities to provide labour for the industrial revolution emerging in massive cities that were almost unliveable. It was also deployed to dispossess native peoples from lands guaranteed under treaty.

New technologies were developed for surveying, in order to map every inch of land into blocks—units that could be traded and speculated on into an infinity of financial abstractions on Wall Street. 'Wall' was an appropriate name for this new ritual centre of the financial system. Blocks of land were walled, fenced and policed by those with a monopoly on violence—physical conflict being another aspect of reality made abstract and legally inaccessible to those without privilege. The fiercely guarded walls prevented the free-flow of humans, non-humans, and various elements essential to the health of the land. The land began to die as a result.

Two thirds of the world's capital is still land today, held by a tiny, privileged minority who can borrow against it as an asset, creating illusory money out of thin air and using it for speculation in a *take-and-take* economy that is paid for by useful idiots who labour endlessly on a treadmill of *give-and-take* 'free market rigour'.

When land became abstracted as walled units of real estate, the culture of the people who had been removed from it also became compartmentalised as 'the arts'. So, there are walls of cultural privilege too, although they are more difficult to discern than those deployed in real estate. Nuanced strata of abstraction are conjured with ephemeral definitions that create distinctions between art and craft, professional and amateur, canon and fodder. Hierarchies are needed to create artistic limitability and excludability through artificially inseminated scarcity. These ranks are determined, as with schooling, through a hidden curriculum of constantly shifting and secretive criteria. The walls are high, the queues are long and there are dogs at the gates.

The further you are from the centre of dominance, the more walls exist between your community and the art that is held at the centre as capital. The powerful encounter a problem here though, related to the annoying remnant of living culture that tethers art to reality. It turns out that art, even in its most abstracted and perverted forms, can only be created by those dwelling in reality, and today those people are the ones who endure life at the margins. At the centre of power, where all the entropy and violence of extractive economies must be outsourced to the margins, reality rarely intrudes beyond the wall. Thus, art cannot be produced there.

Art creation requires a visceral connection to the real world, which is only accessible in this global economic system through suffering. Artists must suffer for their art, or more accurately from the social and emotional pathologies required to produce it. Like all other assets, art is a resource that is extracted from the margins, leaving death in its wake in the form of externalities. Externality is just a polite economic term for people and lands damaged beyond the abstractions of the marketplace and the centre of power.

This is troubling for oligarchs because it means importing people from the filthy margins to make their art-as-capital. If too many are allowed to enter unassimilated, then the centre will no longer be the centre. A game of musical chairs is constructed, offering limited, highly competitive funding to those aspiring to play this game of the arts. They dance around in their millions, hoping to win a seat when the music stops, a golden chair in which they might be hoisted and carried beyond the wall. The winners become human mascots, lauded and paraded to increase the value of the long-term capital they create, until they are used up and burnt out by the excesses and inducements they are showered with, which they consume like sugary treats until they die or become board members to patrol the walls and keep the gates.

Another problem emerges. *High* art cannot be produced by the margins, as that would expose the lie that those at the centre are only there because they are somehow more intelligent, advanced and worthy than others. But how to marginalise a person of privilege at the centre, to confer genius upon them and extract from their suffering and marginality while maintaining their status as one of your own? Fortunately for the powerful, there is a dimension of social space that can marginalise any person, regardless of class and ethnicity, without precipitating downwards social mobility. This is mental illness.

As mentioned previously, contemporary artistic processes produce pathologies. An artist must constantly seek meaning from within, while extracting content and symbols from without. This introspective way of being in contact with place and people turns a person's spirit against itself, poisoning their network of relations and spawning mental illnesses like tumours. This is why so many who produce high art end up killing themselves, developing addictions and occasionally cutting off their ears.

If you examine the spaces in between the oligarchs, investors, patrons, useful idiots in the middle class, the even more useful idiots with middle class aspirations, and the underclasses at the margins, then you will find that the walls containing art-as-capital are the same ones that delineate real estate. Inequality is not an abstraction. It has an infrastructure that is very, very real.

Australia is a lucky country, because it has been able to inherit this extractive infrastructure from its distant emperor. As long as there is something of value to extract from land and culture on this continent, this parasitic nation will continue to enjoy the benefits of its unearned inheritance. The benefits can be seen in the original intended meaning of the phrase 'Lucky Country', which described a nation that was able to gain First World status without having to work for it, by piggy-backing on the vestigial structures of a failing empire and getting good and fat off the teat of rampant extraction.

I'm having trouble with this canoe. I thought carving it was part of my decolonising praxis, but if that's the case how come the colonists like it so much? I should have known I was in trouble the day they became interested in 'centring' my voice. While my voice was squatting at the centre, my spirit, relations and land were falling into disrepair and being stripped for parts.

I came here with tools. It took me a long time to steal those tools and modify them and hide them from my master. It took even longer to find the master's house, so I could use his own tools to dismantle it. Imagine my dismay when I discovered that he no longer lives here. Worse, he wants me to tear it down now, because the insurance pay-out will be even more than he could make from selling it. He wants me to tear it down. He needs me to tear it down. He doesn't live here anymore.

He lives in Estonia now, where he has tripled his fortune selling derivatives, speculating on water rights from my country, which he now owns. He's creating smart cities and a panopticon of surveillance and a brave new Web 3 world with rebooted capital for land grabs in the shadowlands of the Metaverse. I decide to break a window or two before I leave and come up with another plan, but that's when the master's nephew comes to the door to greet me. He's got yoga abs and a nose ring. He tells me he can see my aura and announces that he is my ally now, as he takes me on a tour of all the Indigenous art on his walls. He tells me the skin name he was given when he was 'adopted' by an Aboriginal community in the Northern Territory. He keeps a shaman from South America in the living room and they both give me an uncomfortably long hug and ask me to join them for an Ayahuasca ceremony.

I'm having trouble with this canoe. I've wasted two decades in a post-colonial live-action-role-play, seduced by post-modern and post-structural thoughts and theories, seeking changes to the abstractions of discourse and ignoring the fact that almost everything real exists outside of the text. I've struggled to make change by fighting for more representation in the content that goes over the wall to the centre of privilege. I have neglected even to notice, let alone tear down, the tangible structures of a system that cannot function, cannot breathe without inequality, a system that cannot survive without destroying our lands and Peoples. I thought we had a colony problem, when we actually had an empire problem all along, and the 'we' was a lot more expansive than I ever imagined while I was running around asserting my standpoint and identity and preaching to the converted.

I've been so proud and strong in my exotic echo-chamber, making and critiquing art, innovations and literature for the powerful while the world burned. I see all this in the master's nephew's eyes and I don't feel proud and strong anymore because he *makes me shame* and *makes me weak*. He wants me to help him develop a defi platform on holochain for an online Indigenous artist collective so we can all protect our IP and financially support each other with a new digital currency through this ongoing global economic crisis. He sponsors me to finish making my canoe, and I realise I cannot feed and shelter my children without him.

I'm having trouble with this canoe. I hack away frantically and the wood chips fly like confetti in a celebration of stakeholder capitalism. Canoe-making is a communal process, but I am doing it alone because I'm proud and strong and doing it for my community so we can all be proud of an individual Aboriginal artist's success. I am included. I am special. My voice is centred, but then, what are my hands doing? It is no longer the ancestors who guide every cut, but the invisible hand of the marketplace. This canoe has value because it is rare—it has been years since the last one was made. It is limitable and excludable and therefore can be priced well.

It is a high-risk, extractive activity that involves separating myself from land and community in ways that profoundly damage me. I'm suffering for my art. I am breaking workplace health and safety regulations by refusing to wear protective goggles or use the useless rubber mallet I've been asked to carve with for my protection and safety. I'm decolonising! I'm fighting the power! I'm a rebel! I delude myself into thinking this distinguishes me from every other bastard who has watched a film or read a book in the last thirty years and been radicalised by the propaganda of rugged individualism. Every piece of wood I chip away from this log is a tiny piece of myself. Every cut is a severed relation. But if I double down on this murderous behaviour I have a good shot at succeeding in the big game of musical chairs, entering the top ten per cent in this global economy and maybe, one day, achieving the impossible goal of buying a small plot of our land back.

Deep down, I still recall memories of making a proper canoe.

It began in a place of totemic relation with the waterlilies in a swamp. We were all kin, that species and us. Brolga. Mudshell. Feet, blood and urine. In that place the season was moving us into a cooler time of abundance following a period of heavy rain and the lilies were seeding. We were directed in our connection to this place towards diets and activities we needed to be healthy and complete. There were longer cycles at play too, and above a crocodile nest a tree was flowering that only blooms once or twice in a century. The old people told us that the last time a canoe was made there it was flowering then, too.

While the children played, we caught bait fish and loaded up the boat with water, tools and handlines. We then travelled up river to the site where a tree had been selected to make the dugout canoe. We stopped to pick up aunties who were collecting shellfish and crabs in the mangroves, and the authority shifted to a lady who spoke for the place we were moving through. She told us stories for that river, and we remembered them together.

When we arrived at the canoe-tree site the authority shifted to the old man who spoke for that place. Some of us fished there and I caught a file-snake and some bream for lunch. White birds were diving out in the river so others went out with the boat again to catch the white fish that would be feasting there, fat and medicinal in that season. Women collected gidi beads from a vine in that place and a child learned why it's wrong to be cruel to dogs.

Some of us males took turns to cut the tree down. The old man sang for the tree. We towed the log back behind the boat and stopped at the mangroves to cut wood for oars and outrigging. I learned the names and stories for the rare orchids there. Back at the water-lily place, we ate crabs and then rested for the night.

In the morning the old men started shaping the canoe with axes, digging it out and burning it out with fire. I watched until I knew how to do it and then joined in. We finished making it the next day, and then it was time for the children to do their thing. Dozens of them paddled it around in the shallows and screamed laughing as they did backflips into the water.

We used it a few times after that, but then it was collected and placed on display. It became art. The insect eggs inside the wood hatched and larvae ate it from the inside out. Somebody sprayed it with chemicals to preserve it, but it soon crumbled to sawdust. A mournful blog was written about the demise of 'the last canoe'. It was a priceless asset, lost forever in a sea of dying pillows and 'last of his tribe' narratives.

But that canoe was not a belonging. The belonging was in the relationships that were strengthened in the making of the canoe, the knowledge processes of dozens of activities and stories passed on to the next generation. As long as the relationships last, the maps and blueprints of collective cultural activity will remain as living knowledge that will outlast all the books and servers that might describe the process of canoe-making. I carry a piece of that knowledge, but I can't use it alone, which is why I'm having trouble with this canoe. Intergenerational relationships are the only safe way to store data in the long term, and the only secure place to keep what we now call art. Living culture can only crumble to dust when it is displayed or held in a vault. Art is the death of cultural memory.

I'm having trouble with this canoe. There is tension between the creative source and the extractive activity. There is the caring for community, land and culture that produces these skills in perpetuity (bad for business) and then there is the economic necessity to make products by and for individuals, products that must be limitable and excludable in order to attract a high price. It's nothing personal, but lands and communities must be destroyed in order to produce value. We have to exclude people and cut off relations to value-add the hell out of these products, which are far more than cheap trinkets to mass-manufacture for profit. Oh no, this is art, and these little trophies are to be somebody's capital. These are not commodities, but stores of value. Wealthy outsiders can launder their cash through these unique items. They can even sponsor us to make these things, through foundations that ensure they never have to pay tax on their super-profits.

Boom and bust cycles are for day-traders and wannabes, but art and artefacts are a stable investment for the wealthy, along with gold and land. So here I am, making this object to become somebody else's capital in a way that kills our cultures and communities and land, because the endgame of this process one day will be 'the last' canoe which will be a priceless artefact and store of much value. This reflects a lot of the wrong story upon which our current global economic system is built. Assets only have value when the people and places that produce them are damaged or destroyed in their production, because, my goodness, if every community could make one of these canoes whenever they liked, then they'd be worth nothing at all!

What we had as a custodial species, before abstract nouns like 'art' and 'culture' and 'nature' separated us from the land and each other—these things are still being kept for us. You won't find those things online or in a gallery or some rich bastard's vault. They are kept for us as intangible assets that will never be made liquid, held in distributed intergenerational relations in our communities. You might think they are gone, lost forever if you don't see them on display, but they survive because they are secret and protected. This is the unpaid and unsung work of cultural survival, and it is carried out by people whose names will never be known publicly.

You can't make a living from cultural survival—only from cannibalising your culture to create stores of value for other people's capital. In the arts, we must do a certain amount of that cultural lap dance just to survive, but if we want to outlast this market-driven process, we must keep the most important parts of our cultures private. I'm not just talking about Indigenous people here—everyone needs to do this. Keep the most sacred and meaningful aspects of your culture for your family and community and make sure a significant part of your work remains in the project of cultural survival. People of privilege will eat you up until there is nothing left, otherwise.

Cultural survival will not make you rich or famous. Nobody will ever know you did it, and you will die without that work being praised in your eulogy. But you must do it. You also have to do the other things as well, if you want to eat and be sheltered. Just make sure you have some cultural boundaries and protocols in place for restricted knowledge.

Things are going to get a lot worse before they get better. The extractive economic system we all struggle within for our survival is teetering, but it's far from over. It cannot be tweaked to make it fair for all, as it relies on inequality to function. Its walls are full of white ants and a fresh coat of diversity painted over it will not address the problem. Artists cannot ever be allowed comfort and security, or the machinery of cultural asset production will grind to a halt and the wealthy will lose their investments. Your desperation is structural. You have to be desperate to make the things they want, and they are not going to change things to make your life easier.

Unemployment is also a structural necessity in this system, as it must be maintained and even increased to offset inflation—when too many have the means to survive with dignity, prices for goods and services surge and market instability ensues. This system needs unemployed wretches, including artists, or hyperinflation will burn the system to the ground. So a universal basic income or universal employment policy will not be coming to the rescue for starving artists any time soon.

If you are an activist, which most artists are, don't direct your efforts towards the window-dressing of equity and representation. If you are a minority artist who has spent their career preaching to the converted and has now moved on to molesting the choir—stop abusing your allies. If you are an ally, stop tiptoeing around and pretending there is any moral ground to stand on that is virtuous, or that any space can ever be safe. Are you going to give your real estate back to Traditional Owners? Of course not. As long as land is capital, art will also be capital and we will all be the indentured workers who produce it. If you genuinely want to change this system, the only fight worth fighting is LAND BACK. You might disagree with this, but our species needs a habitat and over the next decade, you'll find out we're all in the same canoe.

Aboriginal and Torres Strait Islander people are not bewildered victims of this global system of arts and finance. We were there when it began, and we have observed its development, choosing where and when to participate, only as much as we have had to for our survival. Other ethnic groups and economic classes have enjoyed more privileges along the way, but in the end our contemporary arts and economies have grown up with the same abusive father and the same battered mother. There is no escaping Daddy though, because there's only one thing he loves better than money, and that's retribution.

So as much as possible, keep your most sacred and worthy cultural practice secret. Don't let money touch it, because Daddy can smell that money and he will track you down.

Render unto Caesar the shit that be Caesar's, and hide your cultural treasures, my siblings.

J'accuse

Australia's great crime against the jobless

The creation and perpetuation of the passive welfare underclass and the urgent need for a universal job guarantee

Noel Pearson

2022 Renate Kamener Oration, delivered at Melbourne University, March 27, 2022.

I honour the Wurundjeri people of the Kulin Nation and bring greetings from Cape York Peninsula.

The descendants of Renate Kamener honour me with this privilege of speaking in her memory as an inveterate champion of human rights. It is fitting my subject today is a human right that near disappeared from rights talk in the last quarter of the twentieth century, and barely resurfaced in these first two decades of the twenty-first: the human right to a job.

Thank you Martin and Larry for this invitation to tread briefly the path of your mother. I will endeavour to emulate some of her fearlessness and conviction in the dignity of all humans.

I thank Larry and my Boston Consulting Group family here in Melbourne and Sydney. Your support is now 22 years long, since I entered the circle of friendship of Colin Carter at a gathering in Weipa at the turn of the century, when BCG first committed to support our Cape York Agenda. Let me thank Colin for his steadfast love. For me and my people, he and BCG have been a great succour to our work.

***

Before making my argument proper, when asked by Larry and Martin last year to nominate a topic for this oration I confess my temper was febrile, because I chose to evoke Zola's 1898 accusations, in the Dreyfus Case, against those at whose feet I will argue responsibility for the needless joblessness might properly be laid. After six months of reflection I have not resiled from my accusations, but let me first accuse myself: for not waking up to this argument sooner. Much effort has been in vain and many lives and futures squandered as long as we have not prosecuted the case for the human right to a job. A human right of all Australians. A human right systematically denied to generations of Australian citizens from the lowest bottom of Australian society.

***

Let me make a second preliminary point about my conviction that Australia's remote communities desperately need a government jobs program—the single most decisive reform if we are serious about the fate of these communities.

If leaders are dealers in hope then the unabating problems of despair in Australia's remote communities, exemplified by the recent media concerning Yuendumu, leaves the nihilists who say 'fuck hope' in commanding authority—because the facts on the ground support them, rather than those erstwhile leaders like me, who try to deal in hope. Yuendemu is only the latest instalment in a decades-long story of despair and long tolerance of misery and destruction of lives.

Little has changed for the better and much for the worse. The key numbers are all worse today than the year 2000. The Liberal National Coalition has been as impotent as Labor in the past.

There I've said it: at the state and territory level as well as the Commonwealth. Each is partly right in their own way. Each is wrong-headed in their own way. Both end up being neglectful and putting the misery of remote communities in the too-hard basket.

And the one thing we have not done is ensured that people in remote communities have the jobs they need to get out of welfare dependency.

From the press conferences we are encouraged to believe Australia has recovered strongly from the pandemic. We are told Australia's job 'generation performance has outpaced every single G7 economy during the two years of the global pandemic' and unemployment is at a thirteen-year low.[1]

But despite the policy insights enabled by the pandemic, Australia is contemplating returning to the past in at least one important respect: a state of affairs in which a significant cohort of Australians are deliberately kept unemployed, so the rest of us can enjoy stable prices. That this cohort is slightly smaller than in the past hides a more complex and ugly reality, because although unemployment has decreased, hours worked have decreased and underemployment has increased. There is an ongoing tacit acceptance that there will always be Australians relegated to permanent unemployment, and therefore poverty and hopelessness.

I too accepted the prevailing economic orthodoxy that tells us we must keep a 'buffer stock' of Australians unemployed to maintain stable prices. I was diverted, along with everyone else, by the ideas that justified permanent structural unemployment for the lowest classes in Australia. I swallowed the fiction that full employment wasn't about every person who wants work having work, but that it was some unfixed number determined by the country's economic managers to be around 95% of the workforce with 5% unemployed—the so-called 'Natural Rate' of unemployment, or NAIRU. I accepted that government could not and should not be an employer of last resort for those for whom the market could not and did not provide jobs. I accepted what we were told were the fiscal constraints on the government's capacity to afford a full employment program. Moreover, I internalised the general disdain with which public job programs came to be viewed; they were 'make-work' involving 'painting rocks' and so on. I had, of course, internalised the argument of the economists about the trade-off between employment and inflation and that managing inflation was the first and last imperative.

The economic orthodoxy, which for too long I took as gospel, was bolstered by the political rhetoric that demonised the unemployed. For close to fifty years, we, the elites who have never had it better for ourselves and for our own families, have been convinced by the policy ideas that permeate the nostrums of our culture—and we have come to convince ourselves and other Australians of these same nostrums—that unemployment is an individual shortcoming. Australia is a country of 'lifters' and 'leaners', we have been told. The leaners are 'dole bludgers', lazy, indolent and ill-disciplined.

This language entered general parlance with the emergence of structural unemployment in the 1970s. 'Dole bludgers' entered the Australian English lexicon at the same time as 'scroungers' in Britain and 'welfare queens' in America. They have little to offer the nation and are happy to suck money from the pockets of hard-working Australians. They could find a job if they just lifted themselves up by their bootstraps.

This all-pervasive narrative not only absolved government of responsibility for unemployment but allowed politicians to direct Australians' fears and economic securities towards those apparently sucking on the government's teat. If only Australia's leaners would do their share of the lifting.

What eludes the authors of this narrative is that there aren't enough jobs for all Australians, especially those without qualifications:

- Over the past fifteen years entry level jobs have collapsed by 50%.[2]
- In June 2021, there were twelve job seeker applicants for each entry-level vacancy.[3]
- It now takes an average of 4.7 years for a young person to move into a full-time job after completing their education.[4]

None of my argument here today is new. Many campaigners for social justice have made the argument for government to step up and become the employer of last resort for the benefit of the lowest and most parlous, needy bottom of society—here and throughout the Western world—to no avail. It was the subject of the last campaign of Reverend Dr Martin Luther King Jnr, who, together with trade unionists A. Phillip Randolph and Bayard Rustin, published the Freedom Budget in 1967, proposing a job guarantee for every American in need of work. This advocacy was continued by his widow, Corretta Scott King—to no avail. As always, Dr King summed up the hypocrisy of the situation the best when he said:

> I believe we ought to do all we can and seek to lift ourselves by our own bootstraps, but it's a cruel jest to say to a bootless man that he ought to lift himself by his own bootstraps.[5]

The truth is unemployment is an economic problem, not a moral one. And the decision to solve it sits with government on behalf of any good society. The Commonwealth has the power to end unemployment for the most needy in Australia, but there has been a bipartisan resistance to using its power.

I have spent more than two decades lamenting what I came to call 'passive welfare'. It was my conviction that passive welfare was a scourge, not just for my people, but for all disadvantaged Australians, regardless of colour or ethnicity—and my convictions about this remain undimmed. It is the central problem that must be solved to tackle poverty and social exclusion in our nation. We must end passive welfare if we want our country to be a great country for all of us.

Furthermore, I always understood the recipients of passive welfare were not to blame for their situation. They were victims of the policy and economic structures that relegated them to the mendicancy of a handout rather than the handup of a job. I know this is not a moral failing as it is too often characterised.

My position is between the old left and the old right on this question.

I agree with the left that the origins of the problem of welfare dependency are structural and that people are not to blame for the society and economy's failure to provide jobs for all. Too many people on the right are in denial about the structural cause of the problem and only want to see it as a failure of personal responsibility.

I agree with the right that long-term welfare dependency erodes personal responsibility and mastery, that it is corrosive to individuals, their families and their communities, and produces family and social breakdown with all of its attendant social problems. Too many people on the left are in denial about the effect of dependency on the collapse of personal responsibility and want to see it as a failure of structural opportunity and of inequality alone. Furthermore, too many people on the left think that the solution is income alone rather than work, which is why there are public campaigns for raising unemployment benefits and for universal basic incomes, but no campaigns for jobs.

The negative intergenerational effects of passive welfare are real. The left's denial of this reality is matched by the right's hypocrisy in blaming the jobless for their predicament while simultaneously running an economic policy that keeps a 'buffer stock' of citizens deliberately unemployed. Let me be clear again: welfare dependency is not the fault of the unemployed. It is a structural problem and, fundamentally, a policy choice. And the best solution to welfare dependency is to provide the unemployed with jobs.

It is no coincidence that the word 'dole bludger' was invented in the 1970s, shortly after the abandonment of the commitment to full employment. Before this, unemployment was seen for what it truly is—an economic problem that could be solved through fiscal and monetary action.

When Prime Minister John Curtin introduced unemployment benefits in 1945, they were not meant to be a permanent destination. They were a temporary safety-net measure that would help people to live in between work and during sickness.

Curtin lived through the Depression and witnessed first-hand the devastating consequences of mass unemployment. To build an equitable and productive Australia, he knew, first and foremost, every person had to be offered a job. It was against this background of full employment that welfare was introduced.

Curtin saw employment as a right of every Australian—he said, 'The Government believes that the people of Australia will demand and are entitled to expect full employment'.[6] And he was willing to use all available levers to create full employment.

It was clear Curtin and Chifley believed that over time social security payments would become less necessary. Why? Because government would use its policy tools and financial power to ensure and create full employment.

This transformative approach led to a period of unprecedented productivity, with an average unemployment rate of 2% into the early 1970s. It was a golden era overseen by governments that used the Commonwealth's financial muscle to bring about growth, productivity and prosperity.[7]

Compare this to the Australia of the past forty years: we have locked out the lowest strata of our society from the opportunities of Australian life. We have come to accept that they will be denied a fundamental right of their citizenship, to have a job and earn a living wage. We have come to believe they are a different species of Australian citizen, who do not need the same opportunities we have. They can live with deprivations that the rest of us would find impossible.

The human catastrophe wrought in the passive welfare era is enormous. Putting aside the original peoples, it would have been unimaginable to Curtin and Chifley, who used the Commonwealth's power to create and deliver opportunity.

In the 1970s, a new economic orthodoxy emerged, marking the victory of the ideas of Friedrich Hayek and Milton Friedman over the Keynesians of the post-war era. Daniel Yergin and Joseph Stanislaw tell the story of how the neoliberals waged a relentless war of ideas against Keynes from the middle of the Second World War. Their 1998 book, *The Commanding Heights: The Battle for the World Economy*, tells how the Keynesian post-war consensus dominated economics around the world. In the 1980s, however, Hayek and Friedman took the commanding heights and became the demigods of economics for the next forty years, unto this day.

Since 1975, Australian policymakers have taken unemployment to mean an unemployment rate of 5%, more or less. But whether this 5% is right or wrong is neither here nor there for elites like us, as the devastation wrought by these policies is of little concern to us.

As John Kenneth Gilbraith is once said to have observed: 'Unemployment is rarely considered desirable except by those who have not experienced it.'

To us elites, the unemployed are not a group of fellow humans left to suffer on the periphery of the Australian economy: they are the economic policy tool of choice in a faux war against inflation. The politicians and technocrats who allowed this social disaster to play out have never been held to account for what was done—and is still being done. They destroyed lives. I could take you on a tour of the graves of many of the victims who I knew and who I loved and for whom I grieve.

They did this so that the rest of us prospered from the economy they presided over. Reflect on the obscenity: the most disadvantaged propped up the macroeconomic system to manage wages and inflation: 3–5% of the country enable the 95% to enjoy the advantages and prosperity that are the right of all Australians but not available to all. Whenever an Australian politician approves of employment numbers that are less than full employment, they are essentially saying that it is acceptable and correct that this 3–5% be excluded from the life-sustaining opportunities other Australians enjoy.

Think about it. The Australian structure of economic prosperity and wellbeing sits on top of a buffer of permanent unemployment representing the bodies of the underclass and their children. These are the people for whom educational failure, poor health, out-of-home care for children, family dysfunction, and juvenile and adult incarceration are at acute levels. This is ground zero of the deaths of despair: suicide, addiction, violence and chronic disease.

This underclass suffers these problems intergenerationally and the country has no solution for them. This much the Productivity Commission admitted in its pre-pandemic 2018 report on Rising Inequality:

> About 3% of Australians (roughly 700,000 people) have been in income poverty continuously for the

> last four years. People living in single parent families, unemployed people, people with disabilities and Indigenous Australians are particularly likely to experience income poverty, deprivation and social exclusion.[8]

What is not admitted is that our advantage sits directly atop this misery. If they didn't help make up the numbers of the unemployment buffer, and if they were not forced to gift their families and their bodies to it, we wouldn't have the system of economic management that has underwritten our good fortune for decades now.

The fact is, public policy choices were made by the Treasury and the Reserve Bank for the underclass: the Treasury decided public job programs were unaffordable, and the Reserve Bank interpreted the data of full employment in a way that could not be more careless of the implications and impact on Australia's poorest citizens. The choices they made spoke volumes for their concern for this underclass. They never saw any value in them. They never saw that the children of the debilitated should have the chance to be free of debility themselves if proper public policy were made in their favour. Why should intergenerational disadvantage be taken to be inevitable, unbreakable and acceptable?

Economist William Mitchell's design of a federal job guarantee, proposing an employment buffer through a minimum wage, makes this story even more sickening. This is what I realised two years ago, reading Mitchell's work: it was not necessary to use an unemployment buffer to manage wage inflation. Inflation could be managed through an employment buffer, using the minimum wage.

For the past thirty years I have watched the devastation of my people from Cape York Peninsula from inter-generational welfare dependency.

The awarding of equal wages for Aboriginal stock workers did not result in the economic equity many had hoped for. Many lost their jobs, migrated to townships and are today churned through unsuccessful employment programs with no real pathways to the mainstream economy.

The 1970s saw many Indigenous people, along with other Australians, moved onto welfare where they stayed for life. This social catastrophe was complemented by the introduction of pubs and poker machines, which allow welfare cheques to be recycled back to government and their corporate friends in these vice industries. Verily, as the black American economist Thomas Sowell once said, 'The poor are a gold mine'.[9]

But my people were not the only victims of the shift away from full employment. Since the mid 1970s the number of long-term unemployed in Australia has continued to rise, despite 30 years of uninterrupted growth for the rest of us.

There are now pockets of suburbs and towns that have experienced 50–70% unemployment over successive generations. All of our communities in Cape York Peninsula fall into this category.

Since the mid-1970s, we, the Australian elite, abandoned full employment with little regard for the impact on the most marginalised—the disabled, the poorly educated, Indigenous people, newly arrived non-English speaking migrants and sole parents.

Australia was never meant to be a country of haves and have-nots. Those who reconstructed the nation after World War II were at pains to ensure that no-one was left out—putting aside the original peoples. They truly believed everyone had something to contribute—putting aside the original peoples. And they designed policies to ensure this occurred—putting aside the original peoples. The dividend was a nation that experienced unprecedented productivity and full employment—putting aside the original peoples.

Please pardon my repeated qualifications here. I have the difficult task of trying to remind mainstream Australians of the golden years of post-war full employment and prosperity for white and migrant Australians, whilst not forgetting that the Indigenous peoples were still excluded from this growth and opportunity. It is the same dilemma Americans have when they remember the great advances made as a result of Franklin Roosevelt's New Deal, whilst having to admit the exclusion of black Americans from its benefits was also the truth.

But allow me to nevertheless evoke the memory of the prosperity of the post-war period for your people, especially the disadvantaged among them.

Regrettably, more than seven decades after World War II, Australia is a country of haves and have-nots. This is not because we had to be, but because of policy choices that were made.

The people of Cape York were the first movers on welfare reform in Australia. We knew it was our right to take responsibility for our future. We got on the front-foot and designed a reform model that focused on building the capability of those on welfare so they could take a fair place in our own land, in our own country, Australia. The people whose dispossession—in the famous words of Justice Brennan in Mabo's Case—'underwrote the development of the nation'.[10]

We designed the Families Responsibilities Commission. Run by local leaders, the Commission builds the capability of those on welfare who have not exercised responsibility in caring for their children, sending them to school, upholding their housing agreements and refraining from violence. The Commission counsels our people and supports them to take up the personal responsibilities which passive welfare has eroded.

Fourteen years on and this model is yielding profoundly important results. Over the past six years in the five communities in which it operates:

- Child protection notices have reduced by 69%
- Tenancy breaches have dropped by 32%; and
- Serious offences have fallen by 23%.

Money management has improved, and parents have saved hundreds of thousands of dollars collectively in Student Trust accounts to cover the costs of their children and grandchildren's education.

The Cape York welfare reform model is working on the personal and family responsibility side of the equation. Personal responsibility is crucial to progress. The other side of the welfare reform equation is opportunity. And in particular the opportunity of jobs. But jobs have not been realised as part of the welfare reform deal.

The results we have achieved with personal and family responsibilities would be amplified if people were provided with real jobs. Over the past fourteen years, job numbers in our communities have remained stagnant. Close to 70% of our people are unemployed. Most live in social housing.

In our original report to the Commonwealth Government in 2007, we argued that the quid pro quo for responsibility and obligations should be opportunities for jobs, education and home ownership.

The gap in Indigenous affairs will only be closed when responsibility and opportunity are combined equally. Attempts to achieve this are non-existent in Australia.

President Bill Clinton tried with the enactment of the Personal Responsibility and Work Opportunity Reconciliation Act in 1996. Let me repeat the name of this legislation because it captures correctly the necessary policy combination: the Personal Responsibility and Work Opportunity Reconciliation Act. The legislation aimed to reconcile the behavioural dimension of personal responsibility in the face of welfare dependency and the structural opportunity of employment.

It is clear this reconciliation was dependent on the availability of work. The deal showed signs of working during the Clinton years of economic growth, when jobs became available, but could not be sustained in the economic downturn. You can mandate personal responsibility but if you leave work opportunity to the market then the reconciliation collapses when there is a downturn. True reconciliation requires the mandating of personal responsibility and work opportunity. If Clinton had done this he would have fulfilled Dr King's vision in the Freedom Budget whose bedrock was a government jobs program. He didn't do it. He mandated only one side of the equation. He was in the grip of the neo-liberal turn in social democratic economic policy thinking, that eschewed full employment as socialist nostalgia, in favour of market solutions. Moreover the pittance of the American minimum wage and the unconscionable way in which workers in the lowest strata of the labour force have to stitch together multiple jobs to earn a living—made the PRWORA reforms a tragic farce.

If we are going to close the gap, not only between Indigenous and non-Indigenous people but between the unemployed and the rest of Australia, we must ensure there are enough jobs for all those able to work and who want work.

Two years ago, I had to confront this great truth. A truth that had never been fully apparent to me. The truth was that full employment was possible without letting the inflation genie out of the bottle. I had swallowed the economic orthodoxy that 5% unemployment was the price the nation had to pay for economic stability, continued private sector investment and high living standards.

That was until I read University of Newcastle economics Professor William Mitchell's proposal for a universal job guarantee. His concept is simple. It is a job for all those needing and able to work. The job pays the minimum wage, superannuation contributions and leave entitlements. It brings the dignity of work to every Australian including the disabled, mentally ill and extremely disadvantaged. And it is a completely superior alternative to passive welfare.

The first benefit of the job guarantee is that it lifts the income of the poorest Australians to a decent level. Only those who have never lived on the dole can say that people can live on the dole.

The second benefit of the job guarantee is that it gives people all of the intangible personal, psychological and social benefits, that come with work. Only those accustomed to the opportunity of work can afford the luxury of the idea that work is not foundational to the wellbeing of all humans.

Mitchell's insight on the government job guarantee came to him as a student studying agricultural economics at the University of Melbourne in the late 1970s, learning the logic of the one-time wool stabilisation scheme. To stabilise the income of producers through the seasonal heights and troughs of the wool clip, and to minimise inflationary prices, the scheme provided for the government to buy the surplus and store it in those ubiquitous red-brick woolsheds near the country's wharves. The retained surplus was released in the years when the clip was poor.

The anguished memory of his working-class father's descent into unemployment had become the young student's life-defining purpose, and he asked himself: if the government could buy up idle wool from producers and release it to the market when demand picked up, why could not the same be done with idle labour?

This was Mitchell's eureka moment, and he dedicated his life to the pursuit of full employment and the concept of a government-funded job guarantee.

The crucial breakthrough Mitchell made with his job guarantee is that its design would mean that full employment with the government as employer of last resort would be non inflationary. He argues there are two ways to manage inflation in employment policy: the first is to use unemployment as a buffer stock against inflationary pressures, and the second is to use employment as a buffer stock. Provided the job guarantee is anchored at the minimum wage, a universally available full employment scheme will not be inflationary.

From Mitchell we have the means to achieve full employment without increasing inflation. This is the third benefit of the job guarantee. It works as an automatic stabiliser in the economy: the pool of workers in the scheme rises and falls with the economic cycle. In a downturn the pool grows and when the labour market picks up the pool shrinks close to zero.

Mitchell has provided a policy solution to the social catastrophe playing out amongst Australia's most disadvantaged. In Indigenous policy in particular, Mitchell has given us the most powerful policy tool to close the gap, not just on employment, but most other gaps dependent upon employment: something which has addled the bureaucrats and technocrats.

Since discovering Mitchell's proposal, I have advocated to all governments for a universal job guarantee.

I have been told in response that:

- The jobs would be unproductive.
- Aboriginal people would just be painting rocks.
- The scheme would undercut private investment.
- It would antagonise the unions.
- It would drain the budget.
- The unemployed aren't capable of working.

But these are not the real reasons for the lack of interest. The real reason is that acceptance of Mitchell's argument would require us—the new elites of the neo-liberal turn—to admit we have it wrong.

It would require us, the new elites of the neo-liberal turn, to admit that we aided and abetted a social catastrophe of enormous scale amongst the voiceless Australians.

It would require us, the elites of the neo-liberal turn, to consider the family breakdown, addiction, violence, misery and suffering that our policies have caused to the voiceless Australians.

It would require us, the elites of the neo-liberal turn, to admit that the unemployed are not innately lazy or defective.

It would require us, the elites of the neo-liberal turn, to admit the government has the fiscal capacity to fund real jobs instead of passive welfare but has chosen not to use it.

And most excruciatingly, it would require us, the elites of the neo-liberal turn, to change the system that has gifted us and our own families significant wealth and power at a time when the unemployed and their families were broken and left bereft.

The reasons we struggle to gain traction on a job guarantee are three-fold. Firstly, so many of us, myself included, submitted to the economic orthodoxy that lower levels of unemployment are inflationary.

Secondly, this orthodoxy suited business, who prefer that, at the lowest reaches of the economy, the scarcity of work should maintain a race to the bottom on wages.

And finally, the political class knows that our social security system does an outstanding job of pacifying the excluded and the disadvantaged, by cutting off their hope and aspiration and giving them the false promise that their secondary services and programs will ameliorate their personal and social problems. And if not, then the tertiary services, in the form of end-stage medical care, out of home care for children and detention and incarceration facilities, can always be expanded.

And it is the passive, not the capable, that neither threaten nor make demands on the political system for a better deal. The unemployed become conditioned to think they are inferior and undeserving of anything better. And they give up.

I ACCUSE successive Australian governments of deliberately confining over 800,000 Australians, who live in families where adults are on the unemployment line where they suffer unnecessarily from poverty, powerlessness and prejudice.

I ACCUSE the Reserve Bank of Australia of not meeting its legislative mandate of full employment—by uncritically upholding ideas about a natural rate of unemployment, they destroyed countless lives, the consequences of which they and their own never have to bear.

I ACCUSE the Treasury of pedaling the fiction that unemployment is natural, inevitable and necessary to control inflation, and resist fiscal intervention in favour of jobs for those Australians in desperate need of jobs, in the name of budgetary rectitude and debt management—but are quick to change their view when a pandemic threatens the jobs of middle Australia.

I ACCUSE politicians of using the unemployed for political gain by directing people's economic insecurity and fears towards the most disadvantaged and away from government itself.

I ACCUSE the industry of job agencies of undertaking a fictitious tick-the-box exercise that does nothing to help the unemployed but instead delivers profits to those who least need them.

I ACCUSE the liberals and conservatives of purveying the term 'dole bludger' and creating the illusion that unemployment is an individual moral problem rather than a structural problem perpetuated by neglectful governments.

And I accuse social democrats and the left for not doing enough to challenge the economic orthodoxy that has so deadened the nation's economic reform aspirations, and in doing so, abandoning the country's most vulnerable citizens who looked to them to champion their cause.

Lastly I accuse myself for not having the policy insight and courage to have said this before.

I implore the political parties of all persuasions, to gather up the moral and political courage to face these truths, to transform our conventional thinking, and to move past the old false orthodoxies. I implore the Parliament and the new executive government in the next term to wield its monetary and fiscal power to guarantee full employment for all Australians.

Thank you.

Endnotes

---

1. Scott Morrison, keynote address, AFR Business Summit, March 8, 2022. Video: 'PM's keynote address at the AFR Business Summit 2022', *Financial Review* https://www.afr.com. Transcript: *Mirage. News*, 'Virtual Address, AFR Business Summit', https://www.miragenews.com/.
2. Julie Hare, 'Young people in skills "death spiral" as entry-level jobs vanish'. *Financial Review* November 8, 2021. www.afr.com.
3. *Faces of Unemployment*, Australian Council of Social Service (ACOSS), 2021, p. 38.
4. Hare op. cit.

5. Martin Luther King Jnr, interview with Sander Vanocour, NBC. Atlanta Ebenezer Baptist Church, Georgia, May 8, 1967. YouTube https://www.youtube.com/watch?v=2xsbt3a7K-8.
6. Commonwealth of Australia, *Full Employment in Australia*, Australian Government Printer, 1945, Part I, p.1.
7. 'Underutilised Labour: unemployment trends and patterns', Australian Bureau of Statistics, 4102.0—Australian Social Trends, 2001. *Australian Bureau of Statistics*. www.abs.gov.au.
8. *Rising Inequality? A stocktake of the evidence*, Productivity Commission Research Paper, August 2018, p. 5. *Productivity Commission*. www.pc.gov.au.
9. Thomas Sowell, *New York Times Magazine*, August 8, 1976. *Foundation for Economic Education*, Document reference no. 812. https://.history.fee.org.
10. *Mabo v Queensland*, no. 2, 1992. 175 CLR 1, pp. 68-69.

About the Authors

ASSOCIATE PROFESSOR JOSEPHINE CAUST is a Principal Fellow (Hon) at the University of Melbourne. She has worked in the arts sector as a practitioner, manager, senior bureaucrat, academic and consultant and has published extensively on arts management and cultural policy. She is a regular contributor to *The Conversation* and the author of several books including *Arts Leadership in Contemporary Contexts* (Routledge 2018), *Arts and Cultural Leadership in Asia* (Routledge 2015) and *Arts Leadership: International Case Studies* (Tilde University Press 2013) and *Governments and the Arts* will be published by Routledge in 2023.

TYSON YUNKAPORTA is an Aboriginal scholar, founder of the Indigenous Knowledge Systems Lab at Deakin University in Melbourne and the author of *Sand Talk*. His work focuses on applying Indigenous methods of inquiry to resolve complex issues and explore global crises.

NOEL PEARSON is one of Australia's leading thinkers. He comes from the Guugu Yimidhirr community of Hope Vale on south eastern Cape York Peninsula, and is the primary architect of the Cape York Agenda. Noel's goal is to enable Cape York's Indigenous people to have the capacity to choose the life they have reason to value by reinstating the rights of Aboriginal people to take responsibility for their lives.

From the Heart
The imperative for the arts
~ the sector responds

Keynotes speeches and discussions from the
Currency House Authors Convention
August 20, 2022 (online)

NO. 3
December 2022

Introduction

The global forces that are transforming our world are rewriting the rulebooks on politics, economics and the environment. Perhaps the most profound change to emerge from this process of 'creative destruction' for Australians is the government's promise to implement the Uluru Statement from the Heart. How will it inform the proposed National Cultural Policy and how will it place 'First Nations first'?

This year friend and former board member of Currency House, Liza-Mare Syron, kindly joined our organising committee to bring together three outstanding keynote speakers for the 2022 Currency House annual Authors Convention: constitutional lawyer Eddie Synot, artist Sally Scales and the Artistic Director of Ilbijerri Theatre, Rachael Maza, to consider the following questions:

> How will the Uluru Statement from the Heart inform the new National Cultural Policy?
> What will it mean for Indigenous performing arts?
> What will it mean for the arts in Australia more broadly?
> What is your vision for the future?

What follows are the edited transcripts of the speeches.

***

Good morning and thank you for coming to the second Currency House Authors Convention. My name is Harriet Parsons and I am the Director of Currency House. I'd like to begin by acknowledging the sovereignty of the more than 400 ancient nations of this continent, which was never ceded, and pay my respects to their elders, past, present and emerging. I am speaking to you from Wurundjeri country and Currency House is on Gadigal land.

I've been asked to tell you a little about our organisation, which is hosting this event, before I hand over to our keynote speakers and Liza-Mare Syron who will be mediating this important conversation about how the Uluru Statement from the Heart will inform our new, proposed National Cultural Policy.

We held our first Authors Convention last year, just for the authors of our long essay series, Platform Papers. My mother, Katharine Brisbane, published 63 Papers by leading practitioners in the performing arts and other experts in the arts and humanities from 2004 to 2021, who were given the brief to:

> define a problem or situation,
> examine its background and causes,
> provide evidence and examples, and
> propose a way forward.

It was—and is—the only publication on the performing arts of its kind, and it has become the journal of record for the national industry and a powerful advocate for change.

We closed down for a year during the pandemic in 2020, and it was appropriate, when we started thinking about reopening in 2021, with myself as the new Director, that we consulted our authors and their wealth of knowledge, on what the future might hold for the arts in the post-pandemic world, and where to next for us?

The theme of last year's convention was imagination economics. It took place at the height of the lockdowns and it was especially dark times for the arts, which had been excluded from most of the government's support programs. But there was also light, because we in the arts could see change was happening. Not little changes in policies and programs here and there, but massive, sweeping changes to the whole idea of what government is for. That revelation, that government was there to support the community, washed over the nation like an epiphany. And that was the hope that kept us going through the pandemic. Since then, the pressure to return to the old ways of thinking has been firm and constant: partly political, but mostly cultural. And when I say cultural, I mean the culture that is the heritage of colonial Australians. Over the past half-century, the nation has incorporated the values of market economics into parts of our lives where they have no place—should never have had a place —and we're paying for it now: in environmental catastrophes, overstretched emergency services and deaths in aged care. And arts organisations have become habituated to those values as well. Habits are notoriously hard to break, and habits of thought especially so, because they are full of assumptions—and the whole point of an assumption is that you don't realise it's there. It is an unexamined truth, a truth that we have taken as given— and a truth that, because it is unexamined, is often false. Our contemporary Australian national culture is underpinned by a raft of false truths that circumstances—fires, floods, pandemic and war—are now forcing us to acknowledge and change.

So, while we contend with the disasters of the present, long-term systemic change is afoot. The waves of 'creative destruction' that are rolling through our economy are transforming our culture in ways that were unimaginable only a few years ago, and perhaps the most profound change for the better that we will see in our lifetimes is the implementation of the Uluru Statement from the Heart.

Our keynote speakers are Eddie Synot, a public lawyer who specialises in constitutional law and an advisor on the Statement from the Heart. Rachael Maza, actor, director and artistic director of Ilbijerri theatre, and Sally Scales, a Pitjantjatjara woman who has worked for the APY Art Centre Collective as a cultural liaison, elder support and spokesperson and is now a distinguished artist in her own right. She is also a part of the leadership team for the Uluru Statement reform.

So, I thank you all for coming today to discuss the implications of the Uluru Statement from the Heart for the performing arts of our First Nations, the Australian arts community as a whole and our changing nation; and for the opportunity to listen.

The Meaningful Expression of Indigenous Sovereignty through the Uluru Statement from the Heart

Eddie Synot

I too would like to acknowledge the traditional owners of the land today in Brisbane, the Turrbal and Jagera people, and thank Harriet, Liza-Mare, Sally, Rachael and the other organisers.

It's a great pleasure, anytime, to speak about the Uluru Statement from the Heart. I am a member of the Uluru Dialogue and a Wamba Wamba man from the Riverina region of New South Wales and Victoria, especially near Deniliquin. As an Indigenous person I am committed to the Uluru Statement from the Heart, and as a constitutional scholar and lawyer I think it is well overdue. I am not a member of the creative arts community, but I hope that what I have to say will resonate with you, as we embrace the change that is coming.

In discussing the Uluru Statement from the Heart, I am going to talk about the potential for a First Nations Voice to Parliament, enshrined in the Constitution, to provide us, finally, with a credible and achievable path towards the meaningful expression of Indigenous sovereignty. I'll be talking about sovereignty, but I will be doing something that, as a lawyer, is perhaps not best practice: I am not going to define my terms or confine my comments to the law.

The meaning of 'sovereignty' is in fact quite nebulous and I want to borrow from this ambiguity rather than avoid it. Indeed, although our constitutional system of governance is underpinned by a rigid concept of sovereignty that we have inherited from the British Parliament, it is not actually defined in our Constitution. An example of this legacy is the role of the prime minister which is not mentioned, despite its importance. Rather, it is established by convention as 'first among equals'. The only roles mentioned in the Australian Constitution are the ministers of state and cabinet itself and the executive council.

But while the meaning of sovereignty is not established in the Constitution, it is defined, in a sense, by our system of government. Sovereignty refers to authority as opposed to power and, especially among democratic nations, it rests with the people. It is this that makes the recent revelation that former Prime Minister Scott Morrison secretly swore himself into multiple ministries so egregious. Our Westminster parliamentary system has conventions of transparency and ministerial responsibility that protect its integrity and by ignoring them and acting on his own authority, he has undermined our democracy.

In a constitutional monarchy both the crown and the parliament borrow their authority from the people: the crown (since the beheading of Charles I) by consent and heredity, and the parliament, through the electoral process. Ostensibly we in Australia have two competing claims to sovereignty by right of heredity over this continent: that of the Crown and of Indigenous peoples. But although the case for Indigenous sovereignty seems irrefutable, the reality is much more complicated.

There are two undeniable and competing facts about the relationship between Indigenous and non-Indigenous Australia that both sides must face up to. The first is summed up in one well known phrase that is much more than a slogan: 'sovereignty never ceded'. It is as simple as that. First Nations have never ceded sovereignty. The land was taken by force and has been retained by force. Many have claimed Indigenous peoples have acquiesced by default. None are correct. In Arnhem Land and other locations, where Indigenous people only came into contact with Europeans in the twentieth century, their law remains the predominant legal system. Those pockets of uninterrupted continuity of law and culture have enabled Indigenous peoples Australia-wide to refuse to be erased, despite the force of the weight the nation has thrown behind it, and to have this conversation today and force this change.

The second, undeniable fact is that the Australian state's legitimacy does not rest upon a treaty with First Nations. This is a fact that is hard for many to swallow. I don't agree with it. I don't like it, but it is a fact that we must accommodate if we are to give meaningful expression to Indigenous sovereignty. The path to change is through understanding and acknowledgment of this fact. Further, First Nations are not recognised as nation states under international law. We do not have what is called 'legal personality'. And it is important to note that the international legal system was authored by those same nation states whose invading colonies are founded on Indigenous lands and now draw their authority from them. So, our rights, even under the United Nations Declaration of the Rights of Indigenous Peoples, a non-binding agreement, are subservient to the nation states within which we have our legal existence. With our acceptance of this system comes the fact that the Commonwealth of Australia is paramount. Even when we enter treaties with the Commonwealth, States and Territories, those agreements remain susceptible to the Australian Constitution and the Commonwealth of Australia. Short of a coup or an entire re-writing of the Australian nation—neither desirable nor realistic—there is no stepping outside of those authorities. It is constitutionally impossible.

These are the political and legal realities we must accept as First Nations. No matter how strong the belief in our sovereignty or how just our claim, those facts will never change. Technical points of law and principles of fairness count for little in the face of history. And this is the context within which we must frame our response. Some see it as intractably difficult. I do not. Although we must work within the institutions of the Australian state, this does not mean those institutions are irredeemably colonial, nor does it mean that we cannot change our nation. The answer is not to accept loss of sovereignty as an inescapable reality—and loss of sovereignty is implicit in those solutions that address Indigenous issues as problems of socio-economic status or 'closing the gap' rather than transgressions of the legitimate rights of First Nations peoples as political and cultural entities. Instead, we need to navigate a pathway through the system that gives expression to what we mean when we say sovereignty was never ceded.

The delegates of the thirteen regional dialogues that led to the First Nations National Constitutional Convention in 2017 understood this. In a process of deliberative dialogue and informed decision-making, they worked through the political and legal obstacles to giving meaningful expression to Indigenous sovereignty and achieving change. This is a key reason why the First Nations Voice to Parliament enshrined in the Constitution comes first in the Uluru Statement from the Heart. Substantive structural reform to the political system has to come first if the Makarrata Commission for treaty and truth-telling is to have meaningful effect. Let's not forget that we have had treaty promises and truth-telling processes before, but in the absence of this structure, they have had little impact on the grander scheme of things. If we are to change the constitutional structure of this nation then we need to begin here, at its foundation, with the Voice to Parliament: a permanent institutional mechanism that respects First Nations by recognising their place in the fabric of government.

Outside of the law, sovereignty has a grander sense that matters to nations on an 'existential' level. It contributes to our sense of who we are—our cultural institutions, our sense of identity, our behaviour. In this grander sense, sovereignty has a much broader and more ambiguous meaning, whether we are using it to refer to our existence as a people, Indigenous understandings or our historical resistance to claims of British and Commonwealth authority over our lands. There is something about this more abstract understanding of sovereignty that escapes the rigid constraints imposed on First Nations claims. It enables two seemingly competing claims by the Crown and First Nations to coexist without contradiction. It lets some creativity into the conversation about where we are heading. Escaping these limitations introduces new possibilities and these have been key to the Uluru Statement from the Heart.

The new possibilities of this moment should not be underestimated. It is a momentous occasion in our national history that after 234 years of the Australian relationship we are finally going to change who we are as a nation and how we relate to one another. It is a moment that takes us forward, whilst keeping us firmly grounded in who we are as First Nations, and as a nation founded on First Nations country. It's new, but it's old; it's about reconciling different entities to create who we will be, going into the future. This is a moment of significant cultural change but one that, in many ways, already exists in who we are now.

I want to take a lead from something in the program today, that the arts are 'the engine of cultural change'. As I was reflecting on this, I thought about the responsibility the arts bear, perhaps more than other areas of Australian society, for our national identity and attitude: how we see ourselves, who we want to be and the expression of all that is, was and will be us. The arts, like many Australian institutions, reflect the troubled history of exclusion and denial of First Nations. These two institutions, the law, and the arts, add context to the denial of Indigenous sovereignty and our legitimate claims, as political and cultural entities, to our lands, laws, cultures, and, fundamentally, our existence as peoples. But the arts, like the law, have also provided the means for resistance, allowing Indigenous voices to speak beyond suffocating orthodoxies. In the face of opposition and denial, especially from politicians—one of the reasons we always end up in the High Court—the arts and the law have allowed First Nations to speak with their own voices. I am careful not to romanticise the struggle of those that have come before us, or read into events more than they warrant, but sometimes, simple expression is an act of resistance. These stories, especially those that challenge orthodoxy and speak for themselves, are a living legacy that is realising its aspirations now, through structural reforms like the Uluru Statement from the Heart.

And here I see the opportunity for parallel changes through the new National Cultural Policy. Amending Australia's Constitution means more than just changing the legal text of the document. It means changing the culture of power and decision-making in this nation. First Nations artists and performers are not voiceless, but recognition of their rightful place in the institutions of the Australian state, including the arts, will give their voices a primacy of place that reflects our rightful status as sovereign peoples.

As a lawyer, I also understand the influence the law has on culture as a parallel institution to the arts that shapes who we are as a society and the place of First Nations within it. Indeed, key to the law itself is a cultural and performative orthodoxy that reproduces and maintains Australian culture. There is not a law course I teach that does not feature the work of Gordon Bennett as a way of describing aspects of the cultural significance of sovereignty to my students that I cannot express, and to which our readings of legal texts can never quite do justice. I have similar feelings towards the reproduction of Sally Gabori's work on the back wall of the Banco Courtroom of the Supreme Court of Queensland. Its towering presence represents Gabori's country and sovereignty over the ceremonial seat of Queensland's judiciary. It is a statement that makes me feel differently every time I see it: about the failures of reconciliation and engagement and about respect for First Nations sovereignty. It is also a permanent reminder of the multiple sovereignties that exist over this country. This important dimension of the changes the Uluru Statement from the Heart will bring in emanates through these examples from the arts.

Some interpret the call for a First Nations Voice to Parliament as implying that First Nations peoples currently lack a voice. Of course, we have a voice, of course we are powerful, and have remained so despite everything we have endured. But we are undeniably, and in fact, voiceless, in the context which the Uluru Statement from the Heart has identified. That context is the relationship of First Nations to the Australian state where our rightful place is denied and decisions are made about us by others. This is the important point about a strong Indigenous Voice embedded in our constitutional structure: it is not monolithic, nor should it be, but neither are we, as the First Nations of this continent, like any other 'minority group'. We are not one among many in Australia. Indigenous interests are different: we are sovereign.

Importantly, however, we are no longer at first contact. This matters for those important strategic decisions we have to take now. We are 234 years into a complicated relationship that is not just about resolving legal technicalities. It's about political legitimacy too and the greater questions that demands. It is much easier to take a principle to the Australian people—a First Nations Voice to Parliament—than to change the fundamental conception of sovereignty that underpins our entire system of government. By choosing this path, we are agreeing to respect the democratic institutions we currently live within, and accept that political legitimacy can only be won through the approval of a certain percentage of the population. But that path does not lead towards a final destination, a terminal point. It is introducing a new principle into our Constitution that will become an inherent part of Australian culture and have the flexibility to adapt and change with us. It is about recognising the realities of the cultural institutions that we live within so that we can change and move forward.

The First Nations Voice—a permanent institution within the constitution, that is fundamental to the makeup of who we are as Australians, taken seriously, not just as one voice among many but as the foundational relationship of this nation—is the strong presence that we need. It sets us up for treaty and truth-telling and empowers us to negotiate. It is key to the legitimacy demanded by First Nations communities, and through it the arts and law may come together to drive the engine of cultural change and transform this nation.

Art, Culture and the Voice

Sally Scales

My journey with the Uluru Statement from the Heart began at the regional dialogue in Ross River. The Referendum Council on constitutional recognition held dialogues across the country and they invited a broad range of community groups to that meeting. Consultation processes in our Aboriginal communities generally involve the senior elders and quite often, only the senior men, so, if you're a young woman, you're not getting a look in. That was what was different about the Referendum Council's consultation process: it opened it up.

I work with the Anangu Pitjantjatjara Yankunytjatjara (APY) Lands Arts Centre Collective, as well as with Eddie and Professor Megan Davis at the Indigenous Law Centre at the University of New South Wales. I started painting not long ago and I'm going to talk about the APY Art Centres, what we do and the unfortunate reality of what I consider to be modern-day slavery among remote artists by unscrupulous private dealers, commonly known as 'carpetbaggers'.

The first art centre, Ernabella, started in 1948, during the days of the Ernabella Mission. Today the APY Art Centre Collective looks after six art centres across the APY Lands, the most recent one in Coober Pedy. We are the only Aboriginal group, that I know of, that has three commercial galleries. My elders want commercial galleries in every State and overseas—their ambition is relentless. There is only one art centre on the APY lands which was started by a brother-sister group, so the art centres were really started by women. For our communities, which are very remote, the art centres are fundamental. They are where our cultural advisors are, where intergenerational teaching happens, and they are also the place where artists have full control and autonomy over their income. They are the only place where artists can make something of their own that does not come from government, and make sure there is food on the table for the young people and oldies in that room and their households. They are also the place where, if you are an elderly person or a person with a disability, you shine. We know how important art is for mental and physical health, and you can see it in those places, where an artist can literally relax. I know that from personal experience.

Last year, 28 of my elders made a submission to the Productivity Commission on the carpetbaggers and this story goes to the heart of what we need from the new National Cultural Policy, so that visual artists in remote and regional areas—desert artists, artists from the Top End—can be protected.

Stories come and go in the media about carpetbaggers: the dodgy dealers of the Aboriginal art world. They always start with a sensational headline and end with quotes from Australian politicians promising action and change. They use words like 'sickening' to describe the carpetbaggers while talking about my elders and their art as national treasures.[1] In 2019 Minister Ken Wyatt, Minister Paul Fletcher and Premier Steven Marshall promised to hold an urgent roundtable discussion with First Nations leaders from the Central Desert, leaders from the regional visual arts industry and their allies in health and family services who deal with the impact carpetbaggers have on our communities. Our letters detailed how grim and chaotic relations had become and we reminded the government again of what this meant for Aboriginal communities on the ground.

Aboriginal-owned art centres are the only source of non-government income, and the only real jobs in our communities. They are a place where culture is celebrated and taught on a daily basis. I often describe them as the beating heart in our communities. The reason we need to protect our art centres is quite simply because we already live with more than our fair share of disadvantage and adversity, including high rates of incarceration, family violence, intergenerational welfare dependence, food insecurity and chronic health outcomes. Art centres represent the opposite: they are full of opportunities and they are the best thing we've got for our communities.

The last time any government attempted to stop the exploitation of First Nations artists was nearly fifteen years ago. The 2007 Senate Inquiry into reports of unscrupulous conduct in the Indigenous visual arts and crafts sector, particularly the unfair treatment or First Nations artists, led to the establishment of the Indigenous Art Code of Conduct. We were told that it would put the carpetbaggers out of business and my elders started calling it 'Art Court'.

It was a couple of years too late for the Western Australian art centres across our border, who had already lost the battle with a notorious carpetbagger whom they alleged had taken over one of its prominent art centres, run it into the ground and then abandoned it. They also alleged that the carpetbagger had taken one of the highest profile artists in that area away from the art centre to Alice Springs, then Sydney and finally their home in Melbourne, where the artist was made to paint for them.

I was in high school when the Indigenous Art Code of Conduct came in, and I was very interested to see how it would change things. The APY Art Centres run by my elders were starting to gain traction and recognition in the Indigenous art sector as well as the wider sector nationally. The art market was booming and the APY artists were benefitting. Unfortunately, the carpetbaggers also took notice and started coming into our communities. One elder was taken from her community in the dead of the night—essentially kidnapped—and we had to bring her back from Alice Springs. Through all these crises, to my knowledge, Art Court has not brought down one of these carpetbaggers.

We are currently living in a time rich with opportunity. Nationally, doors that were previously closed have been opened wide. When Vincent Namatjira won the Archibald Prize, it was a game-changer for our Indigenous artists. It showed that there were opportunities for the young ones coming through, not just in the Aboriginal and Torres Strait Islander art sector, but nationally. We are seeing First Nations artists celebrated in museums and galleries across Australia, and hung next to our other national treasures.

But high-income earners in Aboriginal communities can come under extreme pressure because the level of poverty is so high, and carpetbaggers use their economic and social vulnerability against them. They offer incentives of cars and cash and their pursuit is relentless. They might use a vulnerable family member to lure the artist into a debt that essentially amounts to modern-day slavery. Then the carpetbagger might put up the artist in their home or pay for a hotel and the resulting 'debt' can never be worked off. At the same time, the first debt, from the original family member, also continues to grow. It is similar to the strategies used in sex slavery.

From where we stand, the visual arts industry has given up on the issue of carpetbaggers. The word 'carpetbagger' itself, with its connotations of exploitation, has been replaced by the more benign 'controversial private dealers'. The failure of the Indigenous Code to protect artists from exploitation has been a great frustration to me. Rather than trying to fix the problem, it seems that—as so often happens with Indigenous issues—the parties have quietly agreed it belongs in the too-hard basket.

With the change of language, the focus of the Indigenous Art Code of Conduct shifted onto fake art. Preventing exploitation became about educating artists so that they could protect themselves, and leaders in the arts sector began using catchphrases like 'artist's responsibilities' and 'family responsibilities'. Of course, counterfeiting souvenirs for sale at the Paddington markets is horrible, but the counterfeiters are not putting the immediate health and wellbeing of vulnerable artists at risk. So why did this become the priority? It was the start of a particular kind of victim blaming. The promise that the Indigenous Art Code would put the most notorious and aggressive carpetbaggers out of business gradually disappeared. In fact, since the Indigenous Art Code of Conduct was introduced their numbers have grown. There are now more carpetbaggers and unscrupulous private dealers in Alice Springs than ever before. We know of at least 30 operating in the town itself. What is more, they are becoming accepted in the art world, attending openings and industry events and we are now entering new territory, with carpetbaggers on the invitation lists with our own artists. One of our artists, who won the Wynne Prize a few years ago, was virtually attacked by a carpetbagger, but the police either would not or could not act. So, when the arts industry leaders and the police won't help, we have to turn to pro bono lawyers to get artists out of these contracts, and quite often we end up paying the artist's 'debt'.

At the end of 2019, industry leaders committed to another urgent round table meeting with government. It fell off the agenda with the onset of Covid and hasn't found its way back yet. Instead, I watched as the government held an urgent meeting in Parliament House, supported by both Indigenous and non-Indigenous politicians, on the copyright ownership of the Aboriginal flag. The 'Free the flag' movement had made a lot of noise and they were concerned that its designer, Howard Thomas, was being exploited. But Howard, who owned the copyright to the original flag, wasn't being exploited. He comes from a place of empowerment: he was educated and informed. He was not making decisions under duress, in the midst of a family crisis, or to protect family members that were in immediate danger. Most importantly *Howard was not asking for help.* It is a complicated issue but there was clear decision-making around that flag. My elders have been asking for help for almost twenty years. They have been asking for help to protect their safety and the health and wellbeing of vulnerable artists, and to protect their businesses—businesses that provide the only independent income and real jobs in our communities. Vulnerable and elderly Aboriginal artists are being exploited, now, and have been for the past twenty years. Family members caught in the midst of this horrendous situation are being used as leverage.

We worked hard to create the second boom in the Indigenous art market that fell off the radar during Covid. If Aboriginal artists are to be helped into new opportunities, government must get involved. If our artists are going to be able to scale up their work and grow, and end the disadvantage we live in on the APY Lands and across the Central Desert, government must address carpetbagging. We need proper regulations and we should be able to rely on the Indigenous Art Code and its processes to take action against these dodgy dealers with penalties that have real consequences. This is modern-day slavery. Laws against slavery have been introduced in countries around the world and we need to start considering our own legislation.

My elders and ancestors started this art industry for two reasons: one, to keep culture strong, and two, to generate income and jobs. Young people today are joining art centres, dreaming of their art travelling the world and living a great life on the Land. They feel that, finally, they have something to look forward to, that life can be different from what they have known. And surely there is not a person in Australia who doesn't want that for them.

So how can the Voice to Parliament make things change? My hope for the Voice is that it will create space in the National Cultural Policy for artists to have greater autonomy and control over their lives. Currently the only way for an artist to escape an unscrupulous private dealer is through contract law. The Indigenous Art Code does not protect them. There is no Australian law to protect the artists in our art centres. We need to run these dodgy dealers out the door. Nick Mitzevich commented at the Garma Festival that the National Gallery of Australia was investigating the ethical history behind all its Aboriginal and Torres Strait art works, and valuing any they could not show had been ethically produced and procured at zero. Culturally, they will have value but monetarily they will be worthless. I found that extremely profound. This is not just about educating the Australian people on how to buy ethically produced art, we need an endorsement that says 'this is ethically owned'.

And what does ethical art mean for the individual? I'm a picky person when it comes to buying milk. I buy the more expensive one because I want the farmer to get the best return. I want Australians to understand that the best return for our artists is through the arts centre model: our galleries. We pay an 80% return to the artist. Other commercial galleries pay only 50%. This protects the arts centres and it protects the artists. The APY collective has three commercial galleries and they are a platform for us, especially the younger artists. Without those organisations, we are voiceless. I'm lucky to have an organisation that has such a voice.

I detest the word 'dreaming'. I detest it because for me it is *tjukurpa*. It means law and culture; and I say 'law' not 'lore', because these are rights and responsibilities that go with our sacred sites, sacred songs and sacred dances. It is not something we just dreamed up overnight, it is something that has been embedded in our culture over generations. It is part of our being. Some of my elders will talk about their sacred sites and their cultural areas as an extension of themselves. When we talk about art, culture and law, these things are interchangeable. The National

Cultural Policy needs to protect artists—not just visual artists, but the rights and intellectual property of our theatre artists and musicians—and give them a bigger return; and the Voice to Parliament needs to back the Policy up with law.

For more than fifteen years my elders have been asking for substantial change. I'm not in high school anymore, and we're still fighting for action on the same issues. We just need you to be a little bit braver, a little bit stronger and say 'enough is enough' when it comes to dealing with unscrupulous private dealers.

Endnotes

---

1 See for example Lorena Allam, 'Australia [sic] governments urged to stamp out enslavement and exploitation of Aboriginal artists'. *The Guardian*, https://www.theguardian.com. December 14, 2019.

Re-RIGHT-ing the Narrative

Rachael Maza

I am of Meriam and Yidinji descent, Queensland Torres Strait, and my mother is Dutch. I pay my respects to the country that I am on, Taungurung country, its elders and their ancestors.

I come from a long line of storytellers. My father was Bob Maza, one of the founders of the Black Theatre company, the first modern black theatre company, but of course, there are at least 2,000 generations before him of mobs of storytellers that go way back, and I come at the end of a very, very long line. I hold the baton in this tiny chapter of my life, but this story, told through me as a storyteller and a theatre-maker, goes way, way, way back. Of course, it has been somewhat disrupted recently, by the colonisation of this country 234 years ago.

Black Theatre was founded in the 1960s and 70s very much as a political voice that came out of the 1967 referendum and the movement to recognise Aboriginal and Torres Strait

Islander people as citizens of this country. A wave of support rose up behind it from broader Australia to take that bold step forward. The country was full of hope and possibility, and yet after the referendum nothing changed—that became clear very quickly—but the memory lingered on. And so those four lads turned up outside Parliament House with their umbrella in 1972 and set up the Aboriginal Embassy, and the protest picked up again: 'We *demand* that change!' They lit a fire under the nation and the whole country was protesting:

'NOT. GOOD. ENOUGH!'

The Uluru Statement from the Heart is one of the most profound and inspiring statements to come from the First Peoples of this country since colonisation, and yet there is nothing new in what is being said here. This conversation has been going on for 234 years. There was a major disruption to the First Nations of this country, and we've been fighting ever since.

But constitutional recognition is quite a complex question for all of us. The government first offered a preamble instead of legislation, and I was one of many who thought 'Stuff this shit', when the advertising campaign came out, symbolic recognition is *not* what we want. We are over empty words.

Australia has a long history of empty words and no substantial reform, but this conversation, that has been going on for 234 years, comes in waves, and we're riding a wave now: we can all feel it—it's palpable in the air of the country, a feeling of hope and possibility, but it's like those moments in a story, when a crack in the universe opens up just for a moment—*and we've got to be quick!*

Come on country! We can do it! Let's dive in!

So, it is a very exciting time to be around, because of that sense of hope, that this time it's not going to be just another token gesture or symbolic act. We're actually going to see meaningful change. The nation is going to recognise that we have a special place in this country, that is our rightful place as its first peoples whose sovereignty was never ceded and as the oldest continuous living culture on this goddamn planet. We are not just any old minority group. That needs to be acknowledged first. Everything else flows from there.

So, it's time to stop being cynical and ask, okay, what is this Uluru statement about? I absolutely support its three founding principles:

A Voice to Parliament

A body of blackfellas, sitting at the table alongside government as part of the conversation when any decision that has anything to do with blackfellas is being made. A seat at the table. For God's sake, it's a very, very small ask.

But what does that mean, to 'sit at the table'? We've all been Aboriginal consultants, especially in the arts, and we know what it means for us: you're invited to be in the rehearsal room or give feedback on a script, you give your advice, they cherry pick what they want (if anything at all) and then use your name in the credits.

Consulting is really very problematic but Professor Megan Davis has used a phrase that I could get very excited about: 'a threshold of agreement'. The creative process in blackfella organisations honours and respects those whose story it is. That is the foundation of the process. It is about giving one hundred per cent creative control and ownership of the process to the person or the community whose story it is, and the story sits with them. That means that everything—every decision and the whole way of working—is informed by that principle.

So, for me, the threshold of agreement means the community sitting in a circle, and sitting around in this circle, there are elders, there are songmen, there are dancers, there are women, there's a whole array of skills and expertise. And the expertise that everyone brings into it, whether it's their statesmanship and wisdom as an elder or the talents of a younger person, is respected. There is conversation and a process of listening to each person, hearing what they have to say and through that process, they come to an agreement. They reach a consensus, because the circle has to keep working until everybody is on board. Not everybody is in agreement at the beginning, but there comes a point when everyone is able to accept the position and they can move forward.

This is a way of working that is black-centred. That's not to say that we own it, but I believe that, as a way of making decisions, it is healthier than what we have at the moment, and in the Voice to Parliament, this country has an opportunity to learn from other ways of working. The news that the former prime minister, Scott Morrison, secretly took control of the portfolios of his ministers is the antithesis of what I'm talking about. As I understand it, the Voice to Parliament would sit at the table with government in a process that was respectful, that allowed all voices and expertise to be heard, that would really listen, negotiate ideas and through that healthy dialogue, make its decisions.

For me, that process is the definition of self-determination, and that principle of self-determination is everything that we have been fighting for in black theatre. As a company, it is critical that we have self-determination as story makers, that we have a one-hundred per cent Aboriginal and Torres Strait Islander board and that we are First-Nations led. The process has to be led by us, and the story holders must have the primary place in that circle as the work is made. We're still working out that process, because we're using a Western instrument, this thing called 'theatre', but it's no different to mastering the guitar: we're pretty good at cultural appropriation too.

Makarrata

The second principal, Makarrata, is a big one for me. Here in Victoria, that process has already started and I'm extremely proud of this State's preparedness to embrace what I understand is going to be an unbelievably complex process.

The key thing about Makarrata, for me, is the reciprocal opportunity it offers, if we truly sit at the table together, for all of us to benefit. This concept is just beautiful. The protocol, if I can get this right, is the process of coming to agreement after a struggle. It is hard to get excited about a word like 'treaty', when they have been such absolute disasters for First Nations around the world, but 'Makarrata': there's no English equivalent. Once again, it's the process: sitting around, negotiating and talking. It takes time, it takes listening–deep listening—in *the process of coming to an agreement.* To me, those words are so empowering, so exciting and so needed. How can we get there any other way, after a struggle of 234 years?

Truth-Telling

The third principle, of course, is truth-telling. We have started that process in Victoria, through the truth-telling process with the Yoo-rrook. It is outrageous to think that we could just forget what has happened. It is just absurd. No human being could possibly think that was reasonable, so there is nothing to discuss: we must have this process of truth-telling.

As I reflect on it, this absolutely sits at the heart of what we do in the performing arts. It is all about truth-telling. Ilbijerri was founded thirty years ago by mob from everywhere that had come to call Kulin country home. As they came together they started asking, where are our spaces to tell our stories for our mob? Where is the space where I get to see my stories, our faces up on stage? And that continues to be the heart and soul of Ilbijerri. It is the platform where we get to tell our stories, and it is through our stories that this process of truth-telling happens. That process is critical to the healing of this nation, particularly for those of us whose stories they are, and those of us who have the privilege of hearing them in that shared space.

One example that I'd like to share is the work *Corranderk*, which was based on the transcript of the 1881 Inquiry. Our mob were moved off their lands onto Aboriginal stations, reserves and missions and Corranderk was one of them. It was a way of 'protecting' them: out of sight and out of mind. When these places started, they seemed a million miles from civilisation, but of course then Melbourne started to expand and the government wanted the land back.

But the Aboriginal community was very politically savvy, incredibly sophisticated in their navigation of white man's politics. William Barrak had witnessed the coming of the white man and he mastered not only the English language but the white man's law. So, the community of Corranderk put on their suits and, with their shoes in their hands, walked eighteen kilometres from Healesville to Parliament House in Spring Street to lobby State Premier Graham Barry.

This troop made a petition to the government which resulted in an Inquiry in 1881, and in this extraordinary document the voices of blackfellas have been transcribed. As everyone will be aware, it is very rare thing to hear the voices of the blackfellas of that day, because they weren't considered valid witnesses. They didn't have a voice, but, here in this document, you get to hear the untold story of this Inquiry from 1881, in a whole raft of their voices.

And they won. The government found they could stay on that land and continue to live and work there—but here's the punchline: five years later, in 1886, the Aboriginal Protection Board passed the Half-Caste Act which basically meant they removed everyone except for the old people, as a result of which the community was deemed unable to function. So, they got their way in the end.

There's nothing new in this Uluru Statement from the Heart. What it is asking for, and what is needed for this country to move forward, was said by William Barrack in that campaign. He said:

> We would like the government to leave us here. Give us the ground and let us manage here and get all the money. Why not let the people do it themselves?

It is an extraordinary privilege, as a theatre maker, to be able to create a platform for truth-telling and to tell our stories in a way that is self-determined. It is through the process of telling the truth that that we will break down the stereotypes and 're-right'—make right—the false narratives about us: We are not a dying race. We are not inferior. We are not dysfunctional. In the beautiful words of the Statement from the Heart:

> Proportionally, we are the most incarcerated people on the planet. We are not an innately criminal people. Our children are aliened from their families at unprecedented rates. This cannot be because we have no love for them.

We in black theatre are self-determined in our storytelling, but we are still fighting for space. Why are there only three blackfella theatre companies; and why are there still whitefellas who feel that they are in a better position than us to tell our stories? That is not to say that there's not a lot of goodwill out there, and I would go so far as to say that they all absolutely want to do this right. Whitefellas have used their fantastic privilege to be fabulous allies in this country, but, so long as white institutions—the festivals, the big State theatre companies—think that they are in a better position to tell our stories than us, we've got a problem. The way forward is this concept of self-determination: it's open the door and step aside. Give us your space, give us your opportunities and your privilege, because your profits are made from stolen land.

Make space for us to be self-determined in our story making, because the stories that we will tell, will not be about dysfunction and how we all died out, but about our heroes, our resilience, our extraordinary sophistication and tenacity and political nous and phenomenally powerful communities. The point is, the stories that we will tell, will be our celebration of who we are. The stories that we will tell, will enrich this country. The stories that we will tell, we will share generously with this country, and this country will be the richer for it. And those are the stories that our kids will hear and be proud to be black.

I'll finish on another quotation from the Statement from the Heart:

> When we have power over our destiny, our children will flourish. They will walk in two worlds and their culture will be a gift to this country.

Thank you.

Power, Culture and the Search for Legitimacy

Open discussion mediated by Liza-Mare Syron
Summary and afterword by Harriet Parsons

The law is an intimidating subject, but it has one dimension that is especially significant for the arts and that is the element of culture as its underlying authority. Common law takes its precedents from customs and traditions whose principles and rules of action have been tested over centuries through the myriad cases that have been brought to court by ordinary citizens, to decide how we should properly behave towards one another. As the community's values evolve and new arguments overturn the precedents of the past, culture changes, and so Australia's common law is, in effect, the living code of our customs and traditions.

Despite this, the exact nature of Australia's 'customs and traditions' remains obscure to us, but their values do become apparent in moments like the forthcoming referendum when it is we, the Australian people, who have the authority to change the constitution. It is the values we hold in common, as witnessed by the referendum, that are enacted by Parliament.

However, Aunty Pat Anderson, a member of the Referendum Council, has warned that winning the referendum will be the easy part. The real hard work will start the next day, when it is time to put processes into practice and hold the government to account. At this convention Currency House invited the keynote speakers to think about what those processes might look like and their practical effects on the lives of Australians. This was a different question from the details of the legislation. It was asking how our culture had changed since the Australian Constitution took effect in 1901, and how our current values, customs, traditions and their practices should be embodied in the law and magnified by our institutions.

Eddie Synot answered this question by explaining that Australia's parliamentary system is founded upon convention as much as law, and in the game of practical politics, convention's informal power is strategically more significant than the law itself, because the law provides the principle but it is enacted by convention: convention puts the theory of law into practice. Perhaps this holds the key to the undefined meaning of sovereignty in our Constitution: it is the authority on which the population willingly enacts the laws of its parliament.

Despite the nation's affection for the late Queen, there are few defenders of British colonisation today. Over the past forty years, the balance of moral authority, that defines who we are as a *legitimate* nation, has tipped firmly in favour of First Nations. The tacit recognition of the welcome to country, that has become a unique custom in our culture, inevitably must eventually become explicit in our law, whatever form that might take, and the implementation of the Uluru Statement from the Heart is the first step towards that end.

Constitutional reform therefore begins with changing its conventions and it is important not to lose sight of their power in the complex discussions of legislative reform. They underpin the institutions of society and although they are constructed of language and protocols, not bricks and mortar, their effects on the lives of individuals are no less concrete. The Northern Territory 'Intervention', for example, that built overnight a swathe of brand new police stations in communities that had been begging for resources, help and support, only provided a means to further criminalise them.

Uncle Sammy Wilson, who gave the Uluru Statement from the Heart its name, said in a leadership meeting with Sally Scales, 'I don't think straight in English. I think in my own way. But when I have to change it into English, I lose the way'. Language and customs have structures built into them that can either help us to reach our destinations or 'lose our way'. So, although the speakers at the convention discussed practical changes, such as greater representation of Aboriginal and Torres Strait Islander people on the boards and executive of state companies, more equitable distribution of resources and funding and the creation of career pathways for the next generation, the real solutions were protocols of conduct and behaviour that would reform the culture of how we should properly behave towards one another.

Individuals feel the effects of these changes to their culture as changes in their personal identity. The implementation of the Uluru Statement from the Heart will certainly change Australian identity forever and it is understandable that some should feel unsettled by it. Landscape painting is a particularly powerful signal of cultural identity because it explicitly connects personal identity of individuals to the national culture through its etymological origins in the 'cultivation' of land that evolved over time into the 'cultivated citizen'. Scales, a winner of the Wynne Prize for landscape painting in 2022, described the resistance galleries can encounter when Aboriginal art begins to expand beyond its own 'sector' into the traditional genres of Western art, recounting the reaction of visitors to the Art Gallery of Western Australia who wanted to know where the 'real art' had gone when it temporarily replaced its entire display with works by Aboriginal artists. It is the role of the arts to unsettle its audiences and this exhibition was signaling to white Australians that they do not have a 'sovereign right' to their complacency. She is determined that the *tjukurpa* of the Uluru Statement from the Heart, the Yirrkala Bark petition and the Barunga statement, should never hang together in Parliament House. Bob Hawke shed tears of regret over his failure to deliver a treaty, but Scales retorts, 'I don't need your tears, I need your backbone.'[1]

The exposure of government rorts, pork-barrelling and other scandals has eroded public trust in our parliamentary democracy and there is a saying that 'the master's tools will never dismantle the master's house', but there are many tools in the conventions of the Australian parliamentary system that lie neglected. Arriving at a threshold of agreement, the phrase explained by Rachael Maza, requires careful listening, an open mind and willingness to change, all characteristics of the philosopher John Stuart Mill's much cited 'antagonistic system', in which the meeting between two competing ideas results in the creation of a third that neither party could have imagined alone.[2] Mill's competition of ideas fell victim to an alternative 'code of conduct' that became entrenched in our parliaments by drawing its authority from the 'customs and traditions' of market competition. Under the moral guidance of 'the pursuit of self-interest' politicians were able to defend their actions as 'technically legal' and gradually exclude the common good from parliamentary debate.[3]

Although Australia's head of state remains the British monarch, in reality the authority behind our laws has long been the market place. The Uluru Statement from the Heart is an invitation to all Australians to belong to this country and this land together. This is its gift to the nation: the gift of legitimacy.

Endnotes

---

1 Noel Pearson, 'A Rightful Place: race, recognition and a more complete Commonwealth'. *Quarterly Essay*, no. 55 (2014). https://www.quarterlyessay.com.au.

2. Richard Bronk, *The Romantic Economist: Imagination in Economics.* Cambridge University Press, 2009, p. 40ff.

3. See for example Finbar O'Mallon, 'NSW Premier Gladys Berejiklian says controversial grants program was pork barrelling'. *Australian Financial Review.* November 26, 2020. www.afr.com.

Contributors

Eddie Synot is a Wemba Wemba First Nations public lawyer, researcher and lecturer at the Griffith Law School and Research Fellow at the Indigenous Law Centre at the University of NSW. He works with the Uluru Dialogue, a group of First Nations and non-Indigenous community leaders, law scholars and advocates at the Indigenous Law Centre who run education programs and projects to advance the work of the Uluru Statement from the Heart. His research focuses on Indigenous peoples and the law, especially public and constitutional law.

Sally Scales is a Pitjantjatjara from the Anangu Pitjantjatjara Yankunytjatjara (APY) Lands in remote South Australia. She worked for the APY Arts Centre Collective in Cultural Liaison, Elder support and spokesperson roles, before becoming an artist herself and received the National Aboriginal and Torres Strait Islander Art Awards (NATSIAA) People's Choice award in 2021 and the Archibald, Wynne, Sulman- Roberts Family Prize in 2022. She is a member of the leadership team for the Uluru Statement reform, an independent elected board member of the Australian Childrens Television Foundation and a member of the Alinytjara Wilurara Landscape Board.

Rachael Maza AM is a Yidinji and Meriam woman and artistic director and co-CEO of Ilbijerri Theatre Company. She has performed on stage and screen in milestone productions that include *Radiance, The Sapphires, The Aboriginal Protesters* and *The Dreamers*, and she co-devised and performed in *Beautiful One Day*. Her directing credits include *Stolen, Foley* and *Show Us Your Tiddas!, Which Way Home,*

Heart is a Wasteland and *Jack Charles v the Crown*, which was nominated for a Helpmann Award. Rachael also co-directed *Sisters of Gelam* and *Black Ties* in 2020. She sits on the board of Force Majeure, the First Nations Advisory Board of ACMI and the Indigenous Advisory Panels of Circus OZ and the Australian Opera. She was awarded an honorary doctorate by Curtin University for her contribution to the performing arts in 2019 and is a recipient of the Australia Council Theatre Award.

LIZA-MARE SYRON, family clan Birrbay, is an actor, director, producer and academic. She is Senior Scientia Lecturer at the University of New South Wales and lecturers regularly on First Peoples theatre practices at NIDA. She is a Senior Artistic Associate and founding member of Moogahlin Performing Arts and from 2017–2020 was the creative producer of Koori Gras, a celebration of queer black performance. Her recent directing credits include *God's Country* by Nathan Maynard, commissioned by NIDA in 2021. She sits on the board of Australian Plays Transforms (APT) and her book, *Rehearsal Practices of Indigenous Women Theatre Makers: Australia, Aotearoa and Turtle Island*, was published by Palgrave Macmillan last year.

Take Me to Your Leader
The dilemma of culural leadership

Wesley Enoch

Reprinted from the original series

no. 40
August 2014

You sharpen your axe on the hardest stone.

Kevin Gilbert

Acknowledgements

My thanks are dedicated to my father and the elders of my community who have taught me to be strong and forthright.

Thank you also to Pauline Peel, Katherine Hoepper and Samantha French for your calm advice and constructive feedback. Thank you to David McAllister for the late night conversations and early morning complaint sessions.

A special thank you to Katharine Brisbane (an elder of our community) and Martin Portus for your guidance, editorial eye and steady faith.

Dear Australian Theatre Artists,

What the fuck are we doing?

Where are our leaders?
Where have the rigorous conversations gone?
Where is the sense of engagement in public life?
Where are the voices of dissent and debate?
What has made us so scared?
Why do the arts even matter?

Why don't we speak our minds and make art that excites and challenges the country to be better, be more humane, more ambitious?

What made us so inarticulate?

Do we even know what politics are? No, not party politics, dickhead, I mean the sense of being of the people, the body politic.

Did we ever have a purpose in our communities? Did you? Have we just forgotten it? Misplaced our meaning for a short time? Are we waiting for our brilliance to be finally recognised and for us to be rewarded by the masses without ever talking to them?

What happened to turn us into a pack of whingers and whiners?

What made us so weak?

Every time we say, 'I just want to be an artist' I cringe at the weakness and isolation of that position and think 'What makes us so important that the world has to stop and watch us?'

Toughen up, you weak fucks, and get on with demanding to be seen and heard OR give it up, consider pissing off. Crawl off under a rock and give up.

Am I being too crass? Too hard? What the fuck are you going to do about it? Stop reading? Write a letter of complaint to the publisher? Threaten never to talk to me again? What... go on, what are you going to do?

Nothing?

Your art and your practice is so isolated that no-one would care if you stomped off and threatened never to make work for this ungrateful country again. In fact you might be shocked to find a resounding silence in response.

NO-ONE CARES IF YOU DON'T MAKE YOUR ART.

You may start to fantasise about going to a place that recognises your talents? A sophisticated 'other' world where artists are treated as gods. A place where you don't feel under threat, a place where you have status, a place where you are honoured with milk and honey and manna from heaven. If you think like this... then

YOU ARE DELUDED.

If you want the world to recognise you and love you and cherish you like they do in France or Germany, then fucken' move there. Seriously. If you want it to be 'just like they do it in Europe' then book a one-way flight and GO! If you think you belong somewhere else then get in your boat and sail off into the sunset, make a course for this mythic magical land where you don't come from. You might find that it's hard for everyone everywhere.

I am sick of forever hearing we're not good enough, we don't do enough for artists, we need more money. What have you done to convince our country that your art is worth it?

Who do you talk to?

How are you convincing people that art is important?

Do you talk with people you don't know? Do you broaden your audience? Do you engage with those rare few that want to know what you have to say? Do you work with children? Do you work with old people? Do you ever work with people who are not exactly like you?

Do you ever climb down from your fucking ivory tower to get to know those who are buying tickets to see your work?

How do you ever expect to make a change if you don't get involved with the people who have the choice? Maybe the perfect world for you is one in which everyone does exactly what you want? Where they agree with you and support you unconditionally in everything you ever want to do? A kind of artistic dictatorship where you get to say what the world should be.

Do you really want that? Do you want a world where art and artists are seen as central to Australian life? Do you think creative thinking and imagination is important for everyone in a society? Do you want the lives of all citizens enhanced, reflected and celebrated through art?

THEN, WHAT THE FUCK ARE YOU DOING TO MAKE THAT A REALITY?

Do you want to make this country the best version of itself you can?

Do you want to make the culture of this country one of engagement, debate and civic pride?

Do you want to see a world where the stories that excite us are about us, or give meaning to our lives?

Do you want to create work that transforms, transports and transcends?

Do you want to develop the skills to demonstrate, persuade and convince the doubters of the world?

Dear Australian Theatre Artists,

Do you want the nation to be different to what it is now? Can you see an alternative world? Where are you in it? Where are these visionaries? Artists are amongst the best qualified people to imagine a future, the ones who can carry the creative dreams of a nation. But where are you? I know it's not easy. I know the decision to be an artist does not guarantee the trappings you equate with success or influence but that does not excuse you from articulating a role in making this country the best you can imagine it to be. Are you fulfilling your role in our community?

I'm looking for cultural leadership. Do you know where I should look?

Introduction:
Where does cultural leadership come from?

In Aboriginal society, I was taught, everyone dances and sings and paints and tells stories. You have to, the arts are the way you understand the world. If you don't sing and paint and dance and tell stories you have no way of connecting with your family, your landscape, your history, your religion, your survival. Everybody does it and understands the power of culture.

But every now and then there comes someone who is amazing, transformative and touched by the spirit. They might be the person who can dance like no other, or paints a design that springs to life in front of you, or sings in such a poetic, moving way that it makes everyone listen. When the tribe has someone like that they have an artist. That artist is tapped on the shoulder and told to do that thing and the tribe will feed and shelter them while they continue to paint or sing or dance, or tell the stories. It is a rare situation but this Lore/Law man or woman has a special place in the tribe. They are placed under an obligation to be the best they can, because the whole tribe is relying on them to show them a stronger connection with their History, Land, Culture, People. It is part of a social contract. They have become a cultural leader, someone whom the whole tribe looks to for inspiration as they go about their regular day jobs of hunting, collecting, raising children and the business of the tribe.

In the past few decades this obligation has come to include an economic component. Having an inspirational artist in the form of a painter or dancer can bring economic rewards to the clan. The clan can insist that a painter paints more regularly or engages in the collective painting traditions that see family members making a picture for a 'collectable' artist to sign and sell. The value of the artist within the clan is intrinsic.

I emerged from traditions in which leadership came from elders, gifted storytellers and powerful leaders who engaged in the wellbeing of the clan; and I have lit my fire for discussion and debate from the crucible of Aboriginal community politics. This is not as romantic as it might sound, there are big personalities that live where I come from and they are very happy to put politeness aside and tell you straight. And the notion that there can be consensus on any one issue? Well, you can forget that. It's a form of social Darwinism: you get strong or you get out.

There are so many pitfalls, protocols, personalities and politics to navigate that it can be impossible to understand if you haven't grown up in the culture; but it has given me a thick skin and a solid, iron jaw. I have had to prove my worth within my clan and family, earn the respect of elders and stare down opponents with a will and rigour that I challenge anyone to beat. Some of the best cultural experiences of my life have been when addressing criticism from other First Nations people. *It is invigorating to have to stand up for what you are doing and what you believe in.*

Indigenous people face so many issues—rates of incarceration, gaps in education and life expectancy, housing, cultural maintenance—it seems unholy to be telling stories and thinking it's making a difference. I was marked out from a young age to do something different with my life. Apparently at my birth my great grandmother called me her Methodist Minister and I was expected to do well. Maybe I could be a doctor or a teacher, or a lawyer. When I finally showed interest in theatre my grandmother said to me that there were many ways to heal and teach and practice the law. That has stayed with me and I hold onto the value of my role in the cultural landscape of this country. I have been tapped on the shoulder and the country hunts and collects food and raises children while I am focussed on doing what I can do to reflect and challenge the clan through the stories I tell and facilitate.

As I survey the landscape, the people I looked up to as a young man and learnt from are all gone. Uncle Bob Maza, Uncle Kevin Smith, Aunty Justine Saunders, Uncle Jack Davis, Oodgeroo Noonuccal (I called her Aunty Kath), my father, have passed. We still have stalwarts like Uncle Jack Charles and Aunty Wilma Reading and the next wave of leaders like Rachael Maza, Lydia Miller, David Milroy, Lynette Narkle, Rhoda Roberts, and I am grateful for their guidance and support. They are autodidacts, where no idea is out of the realms of possibility. Cultural leaders are not confined to cultural issues and in fact should have opinions on world events and social movements as well. Leadership comes from wisdom and life experience, skills and that little touch of magic.

But as I investigate the broader Australian community I don't get the sense that we know who the leaders are in the same way. Or the responsibilities of leadership. We have several influential, powerful people in charge of large companies and festivals and arts centres, but I don't know how they engage in leading a community of artists and audiences. Elders of the theatre are often forgotten, thrown on the scrap heap of natural attrition and fashion. The rare few seem to float above it all—Robyn Archer, John Bell, Wendy Blacklock, Carol Burns, Peter Carroll, John Gaden, Roger Hodgman, Liz Jones, Robyn Nevin, George Whaley; but for every person remembered there are untold casts of forgotten.

We all know how tough it is to work in theatre in this country and maybe we are trying to support too many artists. But it is up to those who are working and making a go of it to recognise that to be tapped on the shoulder and given that responsibility of being the storyteller of the clan comes with obligations.

In this Platform Paper I am asking the question: Where and how are our cultural leaders formed? I'm no academic and so this paper is as much about my own journey through the questions and examples of cultural leadership. I'm not that interested in graphs and tables, my interests lie more in thoughts and feelings, provoking some reactions and stirring the pot a bit.

ACT 1—What is cultural leadership?

As another National Cultural Policy, after years of discussion, consultation and representation, seems headed for oblivion due to a change of federal government, do we face the risk that nothing will change? Are we facing a backward slide with the recent cuts to the Australia Council and Screen Australia? Our large companies, festivals and arts centres compete for audiences and funds, pressures increase to pursue greater financial and instrumental returns for government investment, the arguments of under-representation of gender and cultural diversity rage on; we feel increasing unease that those companies and artists with the least resources shoulder the greatest risks, and that arts policy is antithetical to the needs of artists. I come from a theatre background, hence I will be drawing on that experience but there are universal lessons to glean from the specific. I'm sure the discussions in dance and visual art have similar questions, and search for leadership in a similar way.

Are we sufficiently equipped to deal with the needs ahead? What needs to change? Why do we have such an aversion to leadership in this country? Do we have the cultural strength to tackle the big questions?

***

If you read the blogs and management books, cultural leadership is cast as the people in the workplace, their culture and how to create a harmonious workplace to improve productivity and profit. The blogs and purveyors of 'management speak' go on about listening, offering guidance, collaboration, building personal ownership and pride whilst driving towards deadlines, creating outcomes and being efficient. God knows that making art has these elements in spades and leadership in the arts is more than our cousins in the business sector will ever have to deal with.

Leadership in the cultural sphere is more about creating space for the opposing voices, about imagining a future, exploring the repercussions of our values and promulgating public debate through the work we make and the relationships we create. Cultural leadership has come to mean pushing through major evolutionary ideas for the benefit of the nation as a whole. In some of my reading, cultural leadership means simply being in charge of a cultural institution. When talking about cultural leadership in theatre, I believe a broad definition is the most useful. Any person who creates work for an audience has a responsibility to that audience, and therefore should look at their work through a critical lens. If you are not deconstructing the status quo you are constructing it. You have the choice of articulating a progressive or a conservative view of the world.

This progressive/conservative binary can be expressed through form and/or content and much of what is perceived to be leadership is done through the making of work. But I challenge us artists to name a leader who has been articulating their world view through more than their work on our stages. Discussions of structural and cultural change have been next to non-existent in our newspapers, online media and screens. We would be forgiven for thinking that dissent is a secret thing done amongst friends. When was the last time you heard an artist talk about the state of the world? When have you seen an artist expressing anything that didn't seem self-interested or defensive? I can name a few: Cate Blanchett and Andrew Upton have championed environmental issues and Australian values as the joint artistic directors of the Sydney Theatre Company; others have joined the chorus around Closing the Gap and many have stood up for asylum seekers and challenged the detention regimes of our government.[1] However, detractors dismiss artistic commentary as irrelevant or acts of vanity. In 2011 Senator Barnaby Joyce, commenting on Cate Blanchett's appearance in a television commercial advocating for a price on carbon, said: 'I'm so proud of her as an Aussie actor… but this is an area that's got nothing to do with acting.'[2] He dismissed her right to have an opinion and use her position to argue for something she believed was a benefit to the country.

Recent attempts at cultural leadership in Australia have been marked by broad-ranging consultation. Successive state and federal governments have devised strategic plans or policies to shore up support for an instrumental vision of the arts. This consultation often produces lowest-common-denominator policy: it rejects diversity and promotes the building of multi-million-dollar infrastructures to house artistic product, and/or recommends greater market research to inform programmers of better audience development strategies. Though these elements are not 'evil', and I would argue that they are in fact positive steps, they are isolated from the core reasons the arts exist.

The arts exist to reflect the world as it is and as it could be; to bring a new understanding to the world we live in, by exploring ideas, emotions, significant moments in time, personalities and social trends, new aesthetics. But it is also about creating a vocabulary for imagining the future of the world as we may want it to be. Artists are at the heart of this relationship between the 'who we are' and the 'who we might become'. Artists synthesize the ephemeral into something tangible for society and as such are often at the leading edge of societal change. Cultural leaders are those who can imagine this future and bring others together to support their vision.

Artists, by their very nature, are rogues and philosophers—instinctual, naughty, vibrant, edgy, fringe-dwellers who use their wits to survive in a world that pressures its citizens into many shades of conformity. Out of the wonderful circus and vaudeville performance traditions in this country have come our taste for danger and excitement for *carnivale*, the overturning of the status quo, questioning authority and a deep-seated sense of the popular. For thousands of years in this country there has been a balance between the sacred and the profane in performance. Lewd, sexually explicit dances have sat side by side with the most profoundly felt ceremonies. Boxing tent theatrics sat alongside touring opera stars, Russian ballet alongside vaudeville slapstick, imported stars from the UK and US have performed imported repertoire alongside music hall nights and talent shows.

The 1930s brought in the ABC orchestras and the 1950s and 60s saw the birth of a number of companies that would go on to become our flagship opera, ballet and theatre companies. Forward-thinking individuals showed great leadership in seeing them established, and they proved extremely popular. These companies were often flying by the seat of their pants and survived through the indulgence of key figures in government and a loyal public.

In the 1970s, with the establishment of the Australia Council, we saw the formalising of funding support and the growth of some kind of official culture. Funding provided a framework to experiment and explore ideas that examined Australian life and reflected our own aspirations. The question today is whether the idea of state-sanctioned culture has led to the taming and silencing of the rambunctious, dissenting mob that ruled our performing arts for over two centuries. *In the search for the approval of the public purse have we lost our wit and charm, the art of surviving through persuasion, our critical purpose and our taste for the popular?*

Cultural leadership has become more and more about official culture and over the years the leadership has mostly come from government sources. Artists have vacated the field leaving it to governments to take shots at the open goal. Artists sit on the sidelines, complaining that they are not getting into the game and yet they are better placed and more skilled than governments and policy makers to shape artistic practice and the relationships with audiences and society. Whereas in the past there has been a lag between advances in the arts and the policies of government, today we are seeing more of how policy shapes artistic practice.

Artists have found comfort in the official culture, loved being looked after by powerful friends at the centre, instead of embracing our fringe-dwellerness. Artists have been lured by the offer of official recognition, a recognition we have built through consensus, consulting wildly, managing well and balancing the books. But this is not what the arts are about and we should not trust the pressures that ask artists to conform to norms and concede to the status quo.

Do we even trust leadership in Australia?

I believe Australians have a deep-seated mistrust of authority and leadership. We think leaders are lying to us and trying to mislead us. Call it a legacy of our colonial past or blame it on the Australian dream of an egalitarian society, either way our history has made us the inheritors of the tall poppy syndrome, given us unimaginative approaches to policy development and a version of democracy that discourages visionaries and risk-taking. Are we a community divided because of mistrust and our cultural inheritance? Can we ever have strong cultural leadership without 'followship'?

Followship is one of those leadership jargon words that talk about needing followers to build a sustainable movement. There's that You Tube clip that's been doing the rounds. The one of the 'shirtless dancing guy' at a music festival.[3]

He is dancing wildly, alone, without a shirt. He dances with an abandon that is simultaneously antisocial and attractive. His dancing is unique. You laugh at him but you secretly admire his bravery and disregard for those who may judge him. The dancing goes on and on but if you keep watching, at some point he is joined by another dancer. Then another joins in and another. Then these few are flooded by enthusiastic like-minded hippies, gyrating and jerking freely. The clip ends and you move on.

Another version of this clip has a voice-over from Derek Sivers.[4] Sivers talks about leadership and the starting of a movement. He talks about a leader standing alone and having the guts to look ridiculous, making sure that what is offered is simple and easy to follow, being instructional and inclusive. Sivers then says something that sticks with me: that the first follower is a crucial form of leadership; that there is no leader without followers. The first follower transforms the lone eccentric into a leader.

I resist this position only because it makes leadership a kind of popular fashion. Most of what we hail as innovative in this country are copies of interesting trends (mostly from Europe). These trends are as grafted onto this country's cultural landscape, in both form and content, as anything J.C. Williamson brought to our shores, and we are asked to embrace them as relevant and exciting because they come from somewhere else.

I think leadership in the cultural sphere is about articulating a 'truth' that others recognise, a way of thinking that they don't necessarily emulate, but which engages them on some level because it has changed the way they see the world. I worry we have got into a fashion with theatre that dictates the black set or the white set or the perspex box set—a safe kind of artistic leadership that apes international fashion and is only an indiscriminate continuation of our dependence on importation.

There are great artists doing work in this country like Leticia Caceres, Matthew Lutton, Annie Lou Sarks, Daniel Schlusser, Simon Stone, but are they cultural leaders or artistic leaders? An artistic leader can make work which is considered highly skilled and exciting, but I argue that a cultural leader does this *in addition* to making work that is powerfully relevant to our culture. Artists who are cultural leaders must apportion strong cultural value to what we choose to make and where we put our energies. We are not just the first to bring what we have learnt from overseas to our shores. We may convince ourselves that we are being avant garde; but are we just doing what is popular somewhere else? Has our aesthetic judgement become a form of followship, rather than a rediscovery of our own unique ways of making?

I am influenced as much as the next person by what I see and experience when I travel; but the difference is I have a reason for making theatre that goes beyond my own fascinations and personal interests. The need for a story to be told, a sense of urgency or social role, marks Indigenous theatre as different from our non-Indigenous counterparts and I think has lessons to teach all artists.

Cultural leaders mark out contested territory and jump into it. There's been a lot of talk about over reliance on classics and the lack of 'our' national repertoire, the stories that reflect us. There is safety in the known and the risks attached to the unknown are enough to stop resources flowing to the new, transgressive, diverse or radical. These days it seems you can bend, but don't expect to break, the bars of the status quo.

Would a vocal critic like Stephen Sewell ever get produced on our mainstages these days? Would any radical voice find access to the resources of the larger companies and if so under what conditions? It is interesting to remember a time when Neil Armfield, Gale Edwards, Dorothy Hewett, Stephen Page, Geoffrey Rush, David Williamson were radical and new and the systems that were in their infancy supported them to grow into national and international figures. It is hard to believe that this country, as we are now, could create spaces for visionaries; or if we did, that we would replay our history of mistrust. Remember Jörn Utzon and the stories around the Sydney Opera House[5] or Jim Sharman and Lighthouse;[6] or even more recently Peter Sellers and the 2002 Adelaide Festival?[7] Australia has a way of knowing it needs radical creative leadership but loses faith when it comes to backing it up with committed action. We never truly trust an artist to be in charge. Instead we see a growing number of executive producers and managers being entrusted with our cultural institutions. It is difficult for me to imagine a future in which radical leadership could be in charge of any large organisation or social project again.

We, as artists, are the 'lone eccentrics' who are prepared to express ourselves and our ideas regardless of whether they have followers. I would rather be the 'shirtless dancing guy' who is happy being out there on his own than cautiously wait at the edge of the crowd until I feel the wave of others behind me.

But maybe, as a result of our history our leaders choose to stay quiet. Maybe the country has become as suspicious of cultural leadership as we are of the toffs, the pigs, the pollies, the squattocracy, the bosses, the narks, the quacks and other figures of authority.

Cultural leaders, like business leaders, should be articulate risk-takers, inclusive trendsetters, persuasive visionaries and thick-skinned, passionate advocates. I see artistic directorships as more than coveted, well-paid roles within companies and festivals; they are privileged positions that should be occupied by true champions who go into battle for a vision of what the cultural life of this country could be, champions who create the conditions for artistic and creative expression.

Do we have real leaders heading up our cultural institutions and companies? Are we seduced and controlled by the powers of official culture? Do we have champions? What do we need to change to make sure we do? And will we trust them enough to support them when they appear?

Selection processes and governance structures may be instrumental in the lack of cultural leadership and risk-taking amongst our larger companies and festivals. Large amounts of public monies bring with them a sense of responsibility and need for control. Add to this the growing corporatisation of arts boards and accountability to risk managers and there is a hint. The values of those who, by their very nature, are about maximising profit, managing and minimising risk and assessing continuity are becoming more dominant. In an attempt to provide 'sturdy leadership', boards may be selecting artistic directors who reflect these values that are antithetical to artistic and cultural leadership. Companies are becoming extensions of corporate Australia.

ACT 2— Who are our cultural leaders?

If you believe the *Australian* newspaper, and there are many reasons to doubt it, the top ten most influential people in the arts in 2013 in this country were mostly managers, politicians and philanthropists:

1. The audience: viewers, visitors, participants
2. David Walsh: art collector, owner of Tasmania's Museum of Old and New Art (MONA)
3. Simon Crean: Federal Arts Minister
4. Simon Mordant and David Gonski: corporate philanthropists
5. Gotye: singer-songwriter and multi-instrumentalist
6. Harold Mitchell: advertising pioneer and philanthropist
7. Lyndon Terracini: artistic director, Opera Australia
8. Julianne Schultz: founding editor, *Griffith Review*
9. Kim Williams: clarinetist, former media chief, Chair, Sydney Opera House Trust
10. Allan Myers: Chair, National Gallery of Australia[8]

Artists aren't considered that influential. You get the impression that our leaders are those who facilitate artists to make work rather than the artists themselves. It's interesting to see audiences as number one, but I think it has more to do with economics than social ownership. What they spend their money on outweighs the social and artistic importance of the artist. Box-office takings have become a distinguishing feature of what we see as important.

Why is it that influence and power in the arts don't seem to be in the hands of cultural creators? Do artists make effective cultural leaders? The evidence is stacked against us on that point.

The intangible qualitative metrics around artistic value, community wellbeing etc. are very difficult to measure and monitor, whereas the financial and quantitative data around money, turnover, box office, audience numbers etc. are easier to record. This is the key to understanding why we have seen the reins of cultural leadership placed firmly in the hands of people other than artists. The ability to bring money to the table, to assert political power, to manage the resources like a business, are all aspects of our 'show business', but we rarely recognise artistic endeavour as broadly influential.

In theatre we would have to name the artistic directors of the major companies as potential cultural leaders. They are in a position to influence and support grand visions of what is possible in our cultural landscape. Love them or hate them we cannot deny the power and cultural influence of those who built our theatre institutions: Neil Armfield, Alan Edwards, Roger Hodgman, Aubrey Mellor, Simon Phillips, Andrew Ross, Jim Sharman, John Sumner, Richard Wherrett and others.[9] They were the cultural leaders of their day and had the autonomy to grow these companies, artists and audiences.

Do those conditions exist now to support cultural leadership? The measures of success have shifted so much to the quantitative that I reckon artistic directors may feel obliged not to speak out publicly on cultural trends, funding cuts or government policy. Apart from Cate Blanchett and David Pledger, I have not heard any major theatre artist talk about what the cuts will mean for the cultural life of the country.

Attached to the recent funding cuts to the Australia Council was an instruction not to pass the cuts on to the major companies. This pronouncement has cemented in the minds of its critics that, the larger the company the more protected it is from the equitable application of policy. Pledger has called for greater leadership to be shown by the Australian Major Performing Arts Group, the umbrella organisation of the major companies, in light of the cuts:

> AMPAG members take between 65% and 80% of the Australia Council's budget. As of last week, their slice of the pie got a whole lot bigger... AMPAG needs to do the heavy lifting that artists have always done. And I don't mean just cut a bit of fat internally. I mean show responsible sector leadership... The depth of conservatism in the majors is historically counterpointed by the independent sector which consistently delivers on its mission of innovation, experiment, cultural diversity and risk-taking... The solution is not for the mainstream to bring independent artists into their fold, as has been suggested, but to support and nurture their independence outside of it.[10]

This separation, and the tension between the majors and the small-to-medium sector, has deep roots. Natural jealousies, suspicion and envy over resourcing are a given, but there is also an awareness that cultural leadership is happening more noticeably on the funding fringes. Cultural leadership in the areas of gender equity, cultural diversity and Australian stories are being better represented in the small-to-medium sector than on our larger stages.

A quick history lesson: in the 1970s, we saw the rise of the Australia Council for the Arts and the large-scale arts centres; and more predictable support for flagship companies. The major companies were in their infancy, the major arts centres around the country were just being built and the expansion of international festivals was taking off as a sign of growing sophistication. Leadership brought new purpose to the funding and articulation of a Great Cultural Project to wrestle with and explore the power of a national voice on our stages and screens. Around the country excitement rose at the prospect of overthrowing the colonial artistic yoke and embracing our sometimes shambolic, sometimes irreverent, sometimes rough-as-guts voice. Through the Australia Council, new works were commissioned and artists paid to take time out to focus on the making of their art. I don't want to get too nostalgic but it was a time when leaders were born who could articulate their position in the world.

With the 1980s came a period of consolidation, the maturing of skills and refining of arguments. In theatre, writers, actors and innovators like Jennifer Blocksidge, Rex Cramphorn, Jack Davis, Alma De Groen, Max Gillies, Louis Nowra, John Romeril, Stephen Sewell, Brian Syron, David Williamson, Rod Wissler, were hitting their straps and benefiting from the building of infrastructure, funding stability and large-scale audiences.[11] But something happened in the late 1980s and 90s that would change the discussion.

After the stock market crash of the late 80s a new type of economic speak crept into the cultural language. The arts went from being seen as the voice of a nation to an economic powerhouse for the country, in film and television, Aboriginal art and tourist-oriented festivals. We started to see papers on economic impact and multipliers, and we moved from an artistic community to an industry. Our language changed and the arguments we made for support from government also changed.

By the mid-1990s, after an attempt to hold the larger companies to assessment criteria within priority areas, there was a schism. I was on the Drama Committee of the Australia Council in 1993 when we saw the first changes to the selection criteria based on economic principles.[12] The Australia Council had published a number of criteria that we had to address when applying for support. These included diversity, gender representation, Indigenous arts, young people and Australian content; and it was intended that these should be applied uniformly across the applications (though it was understood that any one applicant might not fulfil each of them)—these criteria seem equally important to us today. Then there were the overarching criteria of excellence—to this day this word remains impossible to quantify, but we did the best we could to apply it in a way that was relevant to each application.

You have to imagine a gathering at which the Sydney Theatre Company was assessed in the same way as the theatre-in-education touring company, Salamanca. The criteria were applied and recommendations made, to be sent up the chain to be accepted and ratified. At this 1993 meeting the Drama Committee was chaired by Therese Crea (artistic director of the cross-cultural interdisciplinary performance company Doppio Teatro, from Adelaide). Other members included Stephen Armstrong (general manager of Chamber Made Opera from Melbourne), Sarah Miller (at the Performance Space in Sydney) and a range of other folk including me. (I was working at Contact Youth Theatre in the Aboriginal and Torres Strait Islander program at the time.) This committee had a very broad understanding of the artistic practice of the nation.

So when it came to addressing the published criteria, the committee found that the larger theatre companies did not comply. Their lack of cultural diversity, gender representation and

Australian content was very clear. It appeared that the major companies were not like the other applicants: they always got their money and the application process was a formality. However, in 1993 our committee awarded monies that reflected the criteria. Most of the large theatre companies received decreases in funding of around $500,000. This freed up resources to support a range of other activities across the country. The committee sent their recommendations up the chain.

All hell broke loose.

The boards and artistic directors of the larger theatre companies went direct to government to have the Australia Council return the money that had been taken from them. This was the beginning of the MOB (Major Organisations Board), an unfortunate acronym that soon changed to MPAB (Major Performing Arts Board). This Board removed almost all artistic and cultural leadership criteria from the assessment of these privileged companies. Instead, their artistic criteria were modified with new management and financial reporting measures—but the overarching criterion of excellence remained unchallenged. The larger companies exited the general application process and the dollars they had been receiving from the Drama Committee went with them.

I tell this story not to heap scorn on the big institutions (one of which I now direct) but to explain how a schism of sorts has come to be, between federal funding and the management of performing arts companies today. However, this does not mean that major companies have relinquished their role in leading public debate. I would argue that artistic directors should express cultural leadership from within their companies and through their productions. They should play a crucial role, by seeing a broad range of works, acting as spokespeople for the form, providing analysis and policy advice, advocating for the ecology of the arts.

This should be the bread and butter of these cultural leaders. But to hear an artistic director speak out for a greater cultural vision is rare. In recent times Cate and Andrew have been great at this, Ralph Myers from Belvoir has jumped in to talk about theatre writing and adaptation, Brett Sheehy from Melbourne Theatre Company has been keen to support independent artists through the Neon Season. But there are few voices calling for change, leading the thinking on the big issues. Surely these people are the best positioned to play this role.

Though I am talking mostly about theatre companies, I believe these statements about the nature of leadership are applicable more widely, amongst our orchestras, opera and ballet companies, art galleries, arts centres and festivals. These major institutions are the most secure in our public cultural infrastructure. In most cases the larger organisations are protected through a series of tripartite contracts brought down through the Nugent Report recommendations of 1999.[13] These contracts dictate the amounts and ratios of state and federal support. Cutting back a major company is nearly impossible and requires years of management changes and strict financial stipulations.

Three consecutive years of deficit, management instability, and failure to hold 20% of annual turnover in reserve are some of the reasons for being 'put on notice'. Once on notice, a series of strict procedures are put in place with regular monitoring to remedy the shortcomings. Nevertheless, depending on audience numbers and financial return , these companies are able to pursue and maintain the growth of certain practices, . They undertake riskier and developmental programs as part of their remit—but the major investment of time and resources goes into putting on shows and selling tickets.

Artists, by contrast, live a mostly freelance life going from gig to gig with little security. The rare few who may work full-time in the arts live with the knowledge that sooner or later they will transition out of their chosen field—when their skills wane or their body gives up; or their inability to afford the life others take for granted (buying a house, bringing up children) becomes too much to bear—and they find a 'real job' that remunerates them fully for their skills. The most vulnerable in our community need champions and advocates.

What stops artistic directors from taking on the greater role of cultural leadership?

Artistic directors are relegated by the media to the same human interest profiles as everyone else in the business; and they are asked about their family life, influences and the projects they are working on at the moment. It is difficult to get the air time to talk about a philosophy of making art; or the social role of art or societal issues and debates. But we need to stay connected to the ecologies in which we are operating. Otherwise larger companies can feel removed from the creative debates and discussions and become caught in conservative management rather than culturally progressive models of operation.

This is where I must make an admission. As the artistic director of a state theatre company I have not spoken out. Funding cuts in Queensland in 2013 saw several youth arts organisations fold, and this went by without protest, or even debate, from the larger companies.[14] This was not so much out of fear of retribution from funding bodies, or the need to seek permission from boards, or even the thought that these groups deserved it, it was just a feeling that it didn't affect me. I can make excuses but I believe I thought that it was not my battle. We choose our battles and we spend our political capital in a way that benefits those causes we think are important—in my case Indigenous work, regional touring and new work. At one stage there was a move for the major arts organisations in Queensland to accept a small percentage cut to shore up support for the broader artistic community. This did not happen. I see this now as a lack of leadership on my part.

The artistic directors of the larger theatre companies meet to talk about gender equity, cultural diversity, payment of artists, the royalties for writing in devised processes and adaptations; and you would not find an artistic director who opposed the adoption of these principles. The Australia Council is in the process of changing their grants application format, but through their sector plans you get a sense that the small-to-medium sector is still doing most of the heavy lifting in change and leadership.

ACT 3—Are governments cultural leaders?

Margaret Seares and John Gardiner-Garden[15] wrote a great paper in June 2011 entitled *Cultural Policies in Australia*.[16] The paper maps the history of cultural policies across the federation, the landscape of priorities and processes. It's a worthwhile read to get a picture of changing needs and preferences, but so much has changed today that it is now more of a snapshot in time than a resource for the student of cultural policy. Check out also Hilary Glow and Katya Johanson's paper, *Looking for Cultural Value: Critiques of Australian Cultural Policy*, another assessment of the history of government-led cultural policies over successive iterations.[17]

Governments have been trying to grapple with their leadership role in the arts and culture sector for decades.The raft of separate companies and cultural ambitions are hard for governments to deal with and whenever there is an attempt at a comprehensive policy or leadership statement it seems doomed to be defeated by party politics. I wonder if it is better to think of government as a follower rather than a leader in this sphere?

There are many types of state cultural policy that range from broad consultation and community involvement to unilateral political priorities. When you go searching for something called a cultural policy you come up with so many frameworks, strategic plans and announcements that it is hard to resolve them into one coherent document. An exception is *Arts for All Queenslanders* (2013), started under the Bligh Labor Government and completed under the Newman LNP Government. It is an excellent example of a consultation process which produced a set of principles and priorities for leading decision making. Though it doesn't outline artistic outcomes, at least it gives us an idea of where the policies will be heading in Queensland in the foreseeable future:

OUR PRINCIPLES

Local is where culture counts

Local networks and connectors, local skills development, local opportunities and local products are key to place-making, pride-building, local economy and cultural tourism engagement. Strengthening local communities means strengthening regions.

Participatory culture has landed

Like sport, arts has the potential to enable many people to have a stake in the making, presenting, supporting and discussion of culture. People's active participation in arts and culture and their own creative, artistic and cultural expression is central to strong arts communities.

Quality matters

Along with excellence, beauty and inspiration, people want relevance and value. Quality arts and culture has a connection—a dialogue with its communities. Quality arts businesses and projects continuously learn and improve. Arts and culture that receives public investment must return public value (artistic, cultural, social or economic) to its communities of interest and practice.

Embracing diversity gives us an edge

Diverse cultures, ethnicities, heritage, age groups, abilities, forms, locales and scales of arts practice give us a competitive edge culturally and economically. Connecting with and within this plurality will strengthen our cultural offers.

OUR PRIORITIES

There are four priorities to deliver arts for all Queenslanders:

- returns on arts and cultural investment
- strengthen commercial and entrepreneurial capacity

- grow public value of arts and culture
- strengthen cultural tourism.

> These priorities work together with the principles to determine the types of actions that will help to grow the arts sector, strengthen the community of arts and, ultimately, engage more Queenslanders in more arts and cultural experiences.[18]

New South Wales is undertaking a broad-ranging consultation to create a cultural policy to be released in the second half of 2014. The Western Australian Department of Culture and the Arts is revamping its *Creating Value* policy framework. Arts Victoria has a plethora of policies and program priorities but nothing I could find that gives a one-stop-shop for a big picture view of arts and culture in that state.

***

In October 1994 the then-prime minister Paul Keating unveiled the first ever national cultural policy, called *Creative Nation*.[19] It was heralded as a major achievement, provided an additional $250 million in funding and a broad approach to supporting the arts and artists through a huge range of activities.

This cultural policy was also an economic policy. Culture creates wealth. Broadly defined, our cultural industries generate $13 billion a year. Culture employs. Around 336,000 Australians are employed in culture-related industries. Culture adds value. It makes an essential contribution to innovation, marketing and design. It is a badge of our industry. The level of our creativity substantially determines our ability to adapt to new economic imperatives. It is a valuable export in itself and an essential accompaniment to the export of other commodities. It attracts tourists and students. It is essential to our economic success.

Creative Nation was developed with support from a specially convened Cultural Policy Advisory Panel comprised of film-maker Gillian Armstrong AM, novelist Thea Astley AO, novelist Rodney Hall, designer Jennifer Kee, ABC broadcaster Jill Kitson, Indigenous teacher and performer Michael Leslie, choreographer Graeme Murphy AM, cartoonist Bruce Petty, arts czar Leo Schofield AM and academic Peter Spearritt. In their day, an array of luminaries from a range of disciplines and easily regarded as cultural leaders. They created a Charter of Cultural Rights and pursued the idea of a Ministry of Culture and the promotion of culture to Cabinet-level representation:

> CHARTER OF CULTURAL RIGHTS
>
> We recommend the Government's commitment to a charter of 'Cultural Rights' that guarantees all Australians:
>
> - the right to an education that develops individual creativity and appreciation of the creativity of others;
> - the right of access to our intellectual and cultural heritage;
> - the right to new intellectual and artistic works; and
> - the right to community participation in cultural and intellectual life.

Amazing words. But wait there's more...

> It is time for government to elevate culture on the political agenda, to recognise that it has a natural place in the expectations of all

> Australians. In the light of this, it is important to assert that:
>
> - culture is the expression of a society's aesthetic, moral and spiritual values, indeed of its understanding of the world and of life itself;
> - culture transmits the heritage of the past and creates the heritage of the future;
> - culture is a measure of civilisation, at its best, enhancing and ennobling human existence; and
> - in the Australian context, implicit in our use of the word 'culture' is the value we attach to expressions of a recognisably Australian 'spirit'.

And more. The prime minister said on 10 July 1992, that the Commonwealth's responsibility to maintain and develop Australian culture means,

> among many other things, that on a national level, innovation and ideas are perpetually encouraged; that self-expression and creativity are encouraged; that our heritage is preserved as more develops, and, just as importantly, that all Australians have a chance to participate and receive—that we invigorate the national life and return its product to the people.[20]

The document spells out policy after policy, funding promise after funding promise. It is like a Christmas gift to the country and even now is the most comprehensive commitment to the arts and culture sectors I have read. It is worth reading just to relive the excitement we all felt twenty years ago. It was exhilarating.

But this was to come to nought with the change of government in 1996. John Howard brought us an era of being 'relaxed and comfortable' and we saw many of these developments either disappear or wound back as the 'Beazley black hole' swallowed the arts.[21] The major performing arts companies were protected from many of these cuts and in 1999 the Nugent Report secured their future with a series of fixed contracts between the states and the Australia Council.

It took nearly twenty years before we saw the next National Cultural Policy launched in March 2013, imaginatively named *Creative Australia*. It was based on wide consultation, came with little if any 'new' money, but highlighted some more values and principles to mark the way forward:

> This policy has five overarching goals, developed in close consultation with the community it serves. These goals articulate the future this policy will enable: the centrality of Aboriginal and Torres Strait Islander cultures; the diversity of Australia and the right of citizens to shape cultural identity; the central role of the artist; the contribution of culture to national life and the economy; innovation and a digitally enabled creative Australia.
>
> **Goal 1**
>
> Recognise, respect and celebrate the centrality of Aboriginal and Torres Strait Islander cultures to the uniqueness of Australian identity.
>
> **Goal 2**
>
> Ensure that government support reflects the diversity of Australia

and that all citizens, wherever they live, whatever their background or circumstances, have a right to shape our cultural identity and its expression.

Goal 3

Support excellence and the special role of artists and their creative collaborators as the source of original work and ideas, including telling Australian stories.

Goal 4

Strengthen the capacity of the cultural sector to contribute to national life, community wellbeing and the economy.

Goal 5

Ensure Australian creativity thrives here and abroad in the digitally enabled twenty-first century, by supporting innovation, the development of new creative content, knowledge and creative industries.[22]

This policy was announced with far less fanfare than its 1994 cousin, as the Labor Government rocked with internal disputes. Arts Minister Simon Crean, the major architect of *Creative Australia*, found himself on the backbench after calling for a leadership challenge; and the policy found the bottom of a bin when the election of 7 September, 2013, swept Tony Abbott and the Liberal-National Coalition into power.

In an article in the *Guardian* Ben Eltham wrote hopefully,

> 2013 might be one of the better elections in terms of the arts and culture of many years, with Labor, Liberal and the Greens making positive statements and little sign of the culture wars of the Howard years.[23]

As we now know the 2014 federal budget saw cuts to many of the arts and cultural instrumentalities, including the Australia Council, ABC, SBS and Screen Australia. But Ray Gill warned in the *Daily Review*:

> Where the Australia Council makes its cuts is yet to be determined… but the arts companies most able to absorb cost cutting are spared. Our 28 major arts companies that include Opera Australia, the Australian Ballet and the major state theatre companies and orchestras don't take the cuts. They account for about 65% of the Australia Council annual grants and they are locked into untouchable three-year contracts. The choices left for the Australia Council are to make cuts within its own organisation; to cut individual and project grants which will affect small to medium arts; or do both.[24]

Are governments, therefore, the cultural leaders we are looking for? I doubt it. When it comes to government leadership we find ourselves locked into a disabling flip-flop run on political ideology, ambition and fashion. There seem to be very few policy frameworks that don't come from government and they are all vulnerable to the vagaries of election campaigns and changes of government. Any hope for multilateral recognition of the centrality of the arts and cultural spheres seems doomed.

Some things are too important to play politics with—education, health, and I suggest the arts. Cultural leadership needs to come from those who have skin in the game, who can pilot their way through the complex ethical and social issues. Government, by its very nature, is mired in politics and point-scoring. The intention behind having a ministry of culture, as suggested by the *Creative Nation* Policy Advisory Panel, was to deliver security to the arts, but all it did was paint a target on our backs.

ACT 4—Cultural leadership as ethical leadership

When we talk about cultural leadership we get caught up in policy frameworks and funding, but it can also take the form of protest or an expression of values. As an individual artist, how do you show your values? In theatre this is difficult due to the collaborative nature of the endeavour—each project is made up of multiple individuals negotiating a set of shared values and ethics. I turn to visual arts for the role of ethics in cultural leadership.

The Sydney Biennale

The 2014 Sydney Biennale has been the subject of much conversation around the country, with the withdrawal of nine artists who boycotted the internationally recognised visual art event. Some say it sets a dangerous precedent for arts companies and sponsorship, others celebrate the power of a group of artists to affect a large piece of arts infrastructure.

There is a strong ethical role for cultural leaders to play in leading debate and shaping action, but I wonder whether this has really been an act of cultural leadership or a sign of politics stopping cultural leadership from growing? It is a case of personal perspective for individuals to decide but I reckon it's worth looking at the situation in some detail.

In the Biennale incident the basic chain of events involved a sponsor, a group of artists, a board of management, asylum seeker detention centres on Manus Island and Nauru and a boycott. The Sydney Biennale, a free event, has been around for over forty years, inhabiting a range of venues to showcase the best and most cutting-edge artists from around the world. Alumni of the Sydney Biennale include South African artist William Kentridge, Indigenous artists Vernon Ah-Kee and Brook Andrew and a list of others as long as your arm.

It was set up in 1973 with a major gift from the Belgiorno-Nettis family and the sponsorship of their family-associated company Transfield Holdings. Their website describes the latter as 'a privately owned company with a portfolio of businesses focused on industrial services, infrastructure and renewable energy. It is a huge enterprise involved in large-scale infrastructure projects like the Brisbane Airtrain, Melbourne CityLink, Sydney Airport Rail Link, water treatment plants and a number of public/private partnership projects with government.

The Belgiorno-Nettis family have been long-time supporters of Australian arts projects, and Luca Belgiorno-Nettis, a director of Transfield Holdings, had chaired the Biennale for fourteen years. In February 2014 a Transfield Holdings associate company called Transfield Services won a twenty-month $1.22 billion contract with the Australian Government to operate 'garrison and welfare services' for the asylum-seeker detention and processing centre on Manus Island in Papua New Guinea. The previous holders of the contract, UK security company G4S, had been in charge when asylum seeker Reza Berati died during the violent protests between 16 and 18 February.

Transfield Services already held the contract to run similar operations on Nauru. Transfield Holdings holds approximately 12% of shares in Transfield Services. The Transfield website describes the relationship as follows:

> In 2001, Transfield Holdings floated its operations and maintenance division, Transfield Services, on the Australian Stock Exchange for $1.65 per share. In 2003, Transfield Holdings sold its construction business to John Holland, which is now a part of the Leighton Group. Today, Transfield Services has 27,000 shareholders, with Transfield Holdings having a stake of approximately 12%. Transfield Holdings is no longer the largest shareholder in Transfield Services and Luca and Guido Belgiorno-Nettis ceased their directorship of Transfield Services in 2012. Transfield Holdings does not have a representative on the Transfield Services board and has no influence on the business activities or decisions of the public company.[25]

In February and March 2014 a group of nine artists slated to exhibit at the Sydney Biennale pulled out in protest against the connection with Transfield as a sponsor of the event. The ensuing public debate apparently ended when Luca Belgiorno-Nettis resigned as Chair and Transfield Holdings severed its association with the Sydney Biennale.

From what I can gather, no influence was exerted over the artists in terms of the content of their work, nor any pressure to have their work or themselves associated with Transfield Holdings beyond their connection with the Sydney Biennale. The artists had been invited to create work for spaces as diverse as Cockatoo Island in Sydney Harbour, galleries, arts centres, sheds and other outdoor spaces. In short, the artists were invited to create and exhibit any manner of work that was representative of their achievements as artists. Far from the adage, 'Don't bite the hand that feeds you', the Sydney Biennale has a history of housing some of the most provocative art in the country. So what was the aim of the boycott? To draw attention to the plight of asylum seekers?

On 19 February an open letter from 28 participating artists to the board of the nineteenth Biennale of Sydney was circulated on social media and news sites:

> An open letter to the Board of Directors, Biennale of Sydney
> 19 February 2014
>
> To the Board of Directors of the Biennale of Sydney,
>
> We are a group of artists—Gabrielle de Vietri, Bianca Hester, Charlie Sofo, Nathan Gray, Deborah Kelly, Matt Hinkley, Benjamin Armstrong, Libia Castro, Ólafur Ólafsson, Sasha Huber, Sonia Leber, David Chesworth, Daniel McKewen, Angelica Mesiti, Ahmet Öğüt, Meriç Algün Ringborg, Joseph Griffiths, Sol Archer, Tamas Kaszas, Krisztina Erdei, Nathan Coley, Corin Sworn, Ross Manning, Martin Boyce, Callum Morton, Emily Roysdon, Søren Thilo Funder, Mikhail Karikis—all participants in the 19th Biennale of Sydney.
>
> We are writing to you about our concerns with the Biennale's sponsorship arrangement with Transfield.
>
> We would like to begin with an affirmation and recognition of the Biennale staff, other sponsors and donors, and our fellow artists. We maintain the utmost respect for Juliana Engberg's artistic vision and acknowledge the support and energy that the Biennale staff have put

into the creation of our projects and this exhibition. We acknowledge that this issue places the Biennale team in a difficult situation.

However, we want to emphasise that this issue has presented us with an opportunity to become aware of, and to acknowledge, responsibility for our own participation in a chain of connections that links to human suffering; in this case, that is caused by Australia's policy of mandatory detention.

We trust that you understand the implications of Transfield's recent move to secure new contracts to take over garrison and welfare services in Australia's offshore immigration detention centres on Manus Island and in Nauru. We have attached for your information, a document that outlines our understanding of the links between the Biennale, Transfield and Australia's asylum-seeker policy.

We appeal to you to work alongside us to send a message to Transfield, and in turn the Australian Government and the public: that we will not accept the mandatory detention of asylum seekers, because it is ethically indefensible and in breach of human rights; and that, as a network of artists, arts workers and a leading cultural organisation, we do not want to be associated with these practices.

Our current circumstances are complex: public institutions are increasingly reliant on private finance, and less on public funding, and this can create ongoing difficulties. We are aware of these complexities and do not believe that there is one easy answer to the larger situation.

However, in this particular case, we regard our role in the Biennale, under the current sponsorship arrangements, as adding value to the Transfield brand. Participation is an active endorsement, providing cultural capital for Transfield.

In light of all this, we ask the Board: what will you do? We urge you to act in the interests of asylum seekers. As part of this we request the

Biennale withdraw from the current sponsorship arrangements with Transfield and seek to develop new ones. This will set an important precedent for Australian and international arts institutions, compelling them to exercise a greater degree of ethical awareness and transparency regarding their funding sources. We are asking you, respectfully, to respond with urgency.

Our interests as artists don't merely concern our individual moral positions. We are concerned too with the ways cultural institutions deal with urgent social responsibilities. We expect the Biennale to acknowledge the voice of its audience and the artist community that is calling on the institution to act powerfully and immediately for justice by cutting its ties with Transfield.

We believe that artists and artworkers can—and should—create an environment that empowers individuals and groups to act on conscience, opening up other pathways to develop more sustainable, and in turn sustaining, forms of cultural production.

We want to extend this discussion to a range of people and organisations, in order to bring to light the various forces shaping our current situation, and to work towards imagining other possibilities into being. In our current political circumstances we believe this to be one of the most crucial challenges that we are compelled to engage with, and we invite you into this process of engagement.

We look forward to hearing your response and, given the urgency of this issue, hope that we can receive it by the end of this week.

Thank you for your consideration.

Release of the letter was followed by a boycott by nine (some sources say ten) artists, the resignation of the Chair and the withdrawal of Transfield's sponsorship. Then came a lively debate about the role of sponsorship, public awareness of the issues, recriminations, blame and threats against the artists involved and a general condemnation by government of an arts organisation treating a sponsor so disrespectfully.

I don't wish to dwell on whether this was right or wrong, I believe the individual artists must choose their own way through the web of relationships and associations, but it illustrates the complexities of ethical leadership and reminds artists they are connected to a broader community expectation.

***

I don't believe in such a thing as 'clean money'. All money comes from the process of exploitation, and a decision can only be based on what we can justify for ourselves. Hence, for me, a standard of ethics is personal and founded on individual belief and circumstance.

I recently accepted money from a sand mining company that works on Stradbroke Island (my traditional country). Sand mining has been happening there in one form or another for over fifty years. Native title was awarded to my extended family in July 2011 and the debate on mining has raged, for and against, working for or accepting support from, the mining company. I know for a fact that sand mining has provided a steady economic base for my family for all those years, and that without that financial support my father's family of fifteen would never have been able to stay together in the face of government assimilation policies and welfare laws.

I was conflicted and worried about what sponsorship from this company would mean for a project of mine. On one hand the money could facilitate the project's realisation and enable its artists to reach their potential. On the other, there are deep cultural and spiritual issues connected to the exploitation and extraction of the Land. I talked with my father and other elders. Their advice was to accept the money and use it to promote the stories, people and spiritual and cultural values that the project was attempting to celebrate. I should also use what skills I had to speak up about the issues that were important to me.

So in the end I decided to accept the money of the sand mining company. The project was the play *Black Diggers*, about Indigenous soldiers in World War I. As part of the show we used ochre/pipe clay to ochre up the whole set. The ochre, as it turned out, was purchased from the same company. A fact that interested my elders immensely.

Back to the Sydney Biennale. I wonder what the real options would be, for those of us involved in the arts, when it comes to a sponsorship like the Sydney Biennale? It's worth unpacking the options. What would you do?

1. Boycott or deny participation as artist or sponsor/donor;
2. Accept support from the sponsor; but at the same time create a critical environment within the work or in a discussion about the work that promoted alternative views to those of the donor;
3. Adopt an 'it has nothing to do with me I just make the art' position.

Personally I don't support Option Three. Every artist must be informed about the effect their art may have on their audience and go in with their eyes open. But I can see the merits of the other two.

The boycott has a strong component of censorship built into

it. If a sponsor were to reject a piece of art I made because of its views or values I would be horrified (though it's their money and they can do what they want with it), but does that response apply the other way round? Should artists be allowed to reject a sponsor because their practices don't equate with the artist's views and values? Of course, but I worry that this is an extreme position and is more likely to silence debate than promote it. Option One could lead to suppressing important issues and ignoring, devaluing or excising socially engaged work from public life. The only way to really promote debate is to be part of it and to engage through your work. That is why my preference is Option Two.

I work in Indigenous theatre, so I acknowledge I have a natural inclination to build bridges and communicate with audiences, to promote my position through my work and the associated media that surrounds it. Only through advocating our ideas and our art can we hope to affect public discourse. How can we be cultural leaders if we are not seen to be engaging in the debate through our work? It is no use being just a mouthpiece. As artists our most important contributions come through the synthesis of our values and our work.

ACT 5—What needs to be done?

The general opinion around the world is that cultural leadership defies definition. The very attempt to define a set of skills or perspectives that pertain to cultural leadership slides away into jargon and management speak and corrupts the endeavour. Creativity consultant Pauline Peel says, 'Most cultural leaders reject the term because it seems to have more to do with management'.[26] Lyn Wallis from the Australia Council avoids the attempt to lock it down in her efforts to promote it. In an opinion piece on cultural leadership in theatre for the Australia Council website, she writes:

> At the Australia Council, we know what our artistic leaders, our cultural leaders, look like. They are the 'go to' people, the first names that pop into your head when you need to get communities informed, wrestling with issues, or engaging in serious debate. They bring cool ideas to the big table, and have the strategies to make those ideas play out. Other artists are drawn to them for advice or help, because they know that even if this person can't solve their problem, they'll know someone who can. They hang in there when the going gets tough and know how to take their colleagues with them. Yes, their actions encapsulate all the buzz words. They have incredible vision, they motivate others and demonstrate fortitude in the face of adversity. Most importantly, they possess that intangible gift: the ability to inspire change.
>
> Napoleon Bonaparte said, 'The only way to lead people is to show them a future: a leader is a dealer in hope.'[27]

Cultural leadership is often gained through instinct and timing and pops up like the Harry Potter Room of Requirement whenever a major issue and change and uncertainty rear up. To this end cultural leaders seem destined to learn on the job and avoid the management leadership seminars and formal training around change management. Katie Venner, who co-edited *A Cultural Leadership Reader*, writes:

> As a sector we have an acknowledged preference for learning on the job—experience is what counts… very little has been written on leadership in the cultural and creative sector; we just tend to get on with it.[28]

So what are the areas where we need to build better cultural leadership in Australia and what examples can we learn from?

Write up your stories of cultural leadership

It's rare for Australian artists to share stories of success or ask questions that can affect thinking around cultural issues. Indigenous issues and those of high moral and political complexity, like cultural diversity, asylum seeker policies and gender equity are cyclical and I believe we are destined to neglect them because we act in isolation and rarely succeed in elevating them to become a viable social movement. As potential cultural leaders Australian artists do not spend the time documenting and sharing success stories. We leave the 'bragging' to the media, which it does poorly.

There is no limit to successful projects across the country but we do not put them out there enough. This may stem from a fear of leadership or lack of courage to showcase projects, in the knowledge that nothing is perfect and we don't want to expose our shortcomings. But how can we learn if we hold our successes and failures too close to our chests?

Mentoring and peer learning seem to be the dominant form of support for cultural leaders around the globe. Here is a great example of a UK solution to this form of isolation.

A Cultural Leadership Reader

A Cultural Leadership Reader was published in 2010 by Creative Choices, a UK-based skills and career development site. The *Reader* takes case studies and thinking from around the UK and places them in one convenient publication. Creative Choices is associated with the National Skills Academy, a national network of training institutions. Telling stories of successes and failures assists in peer-to-peer learning and informal mentoring. From cultural diversity and gender equity issues, to management and audience relationship studies, the *Reader* sets out to document the key issues practitioners are facing and trends identified by academics. It acts as a snapshot and repository for current thinking. It has been a valuable tool for me over the past few months.

In some respects the Platform Papers act as a de facto reader on cultural leadership as they document key ideas. Clearer thinking on strategies of cultural leadership is essential to the health of the whole sector. Quotas or no quotas, the issues of female writers and directors, and cultural diversity are worthy of documenting. There is a huge discourse but very little is recorded or publicly available.

How many people know that QTC, La Boite, Metro Arts and BEMAC in Brisbane have housed a theatre diversity officer who has been looking at different engagement strategies with CALD (culturally and linguistically diverse) artists? Or how about the successes and challenges in the employment of female resident directors across STC, MTC, STCSA and QTC? Or the exhibition of stories of Women in Theatre at the Australia Council?

The achievements and discussions on these matters are held in isolation and with very little public scrutiny. A series of case studies showing what we are doing in Australia to address these issues would be a powerful tool. The recording of collective learning and analysis could aid many more organisations and artists to innovate and find what works for them. This could also be a new focus for the Australian Theatre Forum.

In the past five years the Australian Theatre Forum has become an important opportunity through which to address key issues that face theatre as a whole sector. It is the only place that offers a full spectrum of theatre practice and the chance to display leadership. In 2009 and 2011 the ATF was focussed on identifying issues and discussing possible strategies, but by 2013 very little had progressed.[29] The general sense of urgency had dissipated and been replaced by a feeling that little had been achieved. Tempers frayed as long-standing issues of diversity and inequity of resources were aired with, what I considered, a lack of clear direction and moderation.[30] Open arguments, verbal abuse, lazy and undisciplined discussion drowned out reasoned discourse leaving the debate without focus or purpose.

We are destined to repeat past mistakes unless we have a way of recording our attempts at solutions. The history of abandoned cultural policies should teach us to record the principles behind the ideas and inform ourselves. Australia could benefit from a dedicated written record on major issues—maybe a thousand words each from twenty artists on gender equity strategies and the same about cultural diversity.

Multiple records of strategies and case studies would help break the deadlock on these cyclical areas of concern. Or like the recent work by the American group called The Kilroys, an advocacy group for women theatre artists and producers, creating a list of women playwrights and their work.[31] We could easily make a national list of women playwrights and their works that are uniformly praised. It's time to take charge of the discussion and stop the recriminations.

It's time to reimagine what our big companies are for

This has been a theme in my writing. As times change and the role of our larger companies shifts, should we reinvestigate why they exist and what role they should play in our country? If we examined the values and ambitions of our larger companies, maybe we could reassess strategies for their long-term health. Maybe it is unworkable to expect social justice issues to be at the core of large organisations and it is better to release them. I can see a future where some of our larger theatre companies could be given golden handshakes and encouraged to create commercially oriented entities. Surely in fifty years from now, when some of our companies are celebrating their centenary, we will not be expecting them still to be the same.

Local industry support, commissioning and development of new form and new work, training and career development, youth and education deliverables, bench-marking, audience development, developing commercial work... As funding dries up, the larger companies will come under pressure to take on greater responsibility to balance the ecology. But maybe they are not suited to these tasks and should be freed from broader ecological demands. We have a chance to reimagine how these companies work and express their core values and true ambitions to better articulate a future.

At the moment there are mixed messages from governments, artistic communities and audiences, and expectations of these larger companies are confused. They are quickly becoming all things to all people. It's time to look hard at what they are doing, what they do well, what can be done better by others and how the resources are distributed. A deep review, led by the artistic community, could deliver greater artistic returns to the broader community.

This is not unheard of. Not long ago the UK think tank Demos and the Royal Shakespeare Company undertook a four-year project together that saw a wholesale revamping of the RSC.

Demos and the Royal Shakespeare Company

Demos regularly places papers and research in the public domain to stimulate and support creative thinking. Though it does not work exclusively in the arts and cultural sphere, it has done some amazing projects. John Holden is a regular contributor to Demos and was an associate until 2008. He visits Australia regularly as a guest of different arts funding bodies and has been involved in many cultural leadership projects, especially the successful Clore leadership program of mentorships and training.[32]

In 2010 Holden and two associates, Samuel Jones and Robert Hewison, published their work with the Royal Shakespeare Company called *All Together: a creative approach to organisational change*.[33] It followed a four-year consultation process. The publication is free to download from the Demos website and is a story of cultural transformation within one of Britain's most traditional arts institutions.

The book traces how the RSC sought to review the entrenched attitudes within their company and promote the qualities of 'ensemble' beyond the rehearsal room. The company had survived a period of crisis and artistic director Michael Boyd now wanted to encourage the members to embrace the idea of being the best Shakespeare company in the world. Holden points out that from 1999–2002 there were particular hardships in board governance, morale, critical reputation, finances and a strong hierarchical practice in decision-making that prevented innovation and loyalty. Holden and his associates undertook a listening project that delivered the notion of ensemble as a consistent reflection of the core values of the RSC.

The notion of ensemble became the central operational and emotional statement of purpose for the changes and soon began to manifest in the rebuilding of management styles, enabling more inclusion and consultation in decision making, from employment to repertoire choices, engaging with the local community, modifying the theatres to promote connection with the audience and creating more equitable pay scales and travel conditions (the artistic director gave up his chauffeured car). The result of this process saw increases in box-office revenue, reputation and morale and noticeably improved job satisfaction. It is worth reading this paper to see how an organisation, with over 800 staff, can address change and provide better outcomes.

Our larger companies are at a similar crossroads to the RSC. Opera companies are in need of a reboot, as we see our flagship opera company build its tourism and commercial arms to rival its regular in-theatre offerings; orchestras have been in flux since many were devolved from the ABC almost a decade ago; dance companies either want to grow in size or spend a great deal of time touring; and theatre companies are in greater competition with festivals and arts centres.

It is time to have a long look at the models that have been

inherited and imagine different futures. Post-Nugent these companies need revamping. The Australia Council's Artistic Vibrancy program went some way towards addressing this but is was small scale and totally voluntary. Its program of self-analysis suggested strategies for greater connection with the artistic community.[34] At QTC this resulted in a series of measures including a ten-person Associate Artists gathering to assess standards and programming ideas, a group of resident artists, an Indigenous Reference Group, a formal appraisal process for each activity, key performance indicators around gender, cultural diversity, Australian content, critical reception, audience attendance and financial outcomes. There is a culture of mindfulness and data recording but I think it's time for a big chat about where we think these companies will be in fifty years and what their core values are.

There is no use demanding a leopard change its spots, better to recognise the beast and teach it to be the best version of itself it can be. New models of management and ways of talking to audiences would be more possible if we took the time to reimagine how the large companies operate and how they fit into the ecology. Imagine a world where crowd-funding replaced subscriptions or where the relationship between arts centres and producing companies was more fluid. Maybe the future is not about having flagship producing companies at all but a market where arts centres and venues run audience-focussed subscriptions and producing companies spend their time selling their shows to venues, festivals and touring organisations. It would take an act of cultural leadership... Instead we see many of our larger companies engaged in survival and self-preservation.

Create sustainable careers, succession planning for artists and separate the training of artists from university models

The training of artists was traditionally an apprenticeship model within companies of actors but from the 1950s we began to see the rise of our training schools. Today these schools graduate close to 300 students a year and a high level of attrition is accepted within these graduating cohorts. Everyone has a story of a hopeful graduate who moves to Sydney to serve coffee while they wait to get a gig, until they chuck it in and bin their dreams.

Though there is merit in the argument that foundation disciplines form the core of any secondary career (actors going on to become lawyers, set designers becoming industrial design workers) there are limited returns for the cultural life of our country. The financial pressures on universities are creating tensions between quantity of student intake and quality of training. Conservatory style teaching is expensive. It's time to reinvigorate the relationship with training institutions. *I believe it is time companies took on groups of apprentices to train and perform as part of a company of artists.*

We have to create environments where artists think practically and creatively to build long-term sustainable careers. The skills learnt within a creative training course are applicable to a wide range of outcomes but there are very few models that train artists to think about where their skills could be used differently. These adaptations are taking place naturally amongst the armies of 'failed' artists, but I don't believe that training courses are keeping up. There is a lack of entrepreneurial training that could see transition and succession become a more positive experience for arts-trained graduates. If high levels of attrition are the norm we need to reappraise our training course to better serve the individual and instil the skills and perspectives that help build sustainable careers.

Kaospilot

Kaospilot is a Danish training school focused on creativity and innovation. The course work is practical and the curriculum is certified through the Aarhus School of Business. The articulated purpose of Kaospilot is to create 'positive societal change through personal growth' I was introduced to them by Michael and Ludmila Doneman when I was working at Contact Youth Theatre. Their mix of social enterprise, empowerment of students and creative problem-solving has made them leaders in the field.

Michael and Ludmila have gone on to establish a company called Edgeware that works in similar areas of training and social enterprise. Both Edgeware and Kaospilot come from the same DNA of marrying understanding of audiences, artistic skills and creative problem-solving with a deep entrepreneurial spirit:

> A Kaospilot is an enterprising leader who navigates change for the benefit of him/herself and society as a whole. The Kaospilot navigates terrain. They take the unknown and make it theirs. Beyond navigation, they help to give form to the very ground. This involves redefinition of norms. Stepping outside conventional thinking. The Kaospilot dares. They strike into things beyond, not thought of, never dreamed. The Kaospilot is responsible for building the dreams of the next millennium. Their strength is a process of innovation, invention, and improvisation. They play off of situations. They seem to master a fluency in human potential. The Kaospilot invites everyone to step

> beyond their boundaries. What they know is to not work to expectations. Instead, they throw far afield. That anything is possible. And that once they think it, they can find a way to get there.
>
> William Tate, Umbau[35]

Projects undertaken by Kaospilot alumni include the setting up of youth arts spaces; industrial design outcomes as diverse as stationery, shoes, and imaginative car detailing; and a wonderful array of social experimentation around sustainability and cultural shifts in thinking about community.

I was told about one project that involved a local council choosing a new series of buses for the town. The bus options were already in use in different parts of Europe, so as part of the public consultation they selected a range of buses and their drivers from those cities and brought them to the town. For several weeks the foreign drivers drove their buses around the streets and gathered opinion from residents. The project succeeded in animating what could have been a mundane task for local government and turned it into a social experiment in adventure and novelty.

Here are some other examples of creative thinking: in 2009 Kaospilot graduate Henrique Vedana created the Magic Kombi in response to the need for more communication between eco-enterprises and sustainability initiatives in South America. The Magic Kombi was modified and decked out with environmentally friendly technologies to showcase low-impact lifestyle options. A website and blog were created to house the research and the networks that were created.[36] The Magic Kombi created a sense of adventure and performance, documenting stories and sharing experiences. The outcomes of the project included establishing communication between eco-villages and initiatives across the globe, the showcasing of new technologies throughout South America and the establishment of business cases for new environmental projects.

Recent Kaospilot graduates have devised projects like *Skateducate*, a skate boarding initiative for young girls to bridge social and cultural divides; *Dance for Love*, a cross-cultural dance project that has now become a national day in Sweden; *Game Changer Game Jam* which brings together gamers to gamify social, political and environmental challenges to create better connections between online and real world issues; *Trinitas* which looks at the role of dogs in assisting people with mental challenges and puts dogs in libraries for children with reading difficulties and anxiety...[37] The list goes on.

Kaospilot sees change and uncertainty as an opportunity to build social capital and, far from being hemmed in by the arts, embraces opportunities for creative thinking in every sphere of life and work. Practical problem-solving through creative projects could create more connection between the society we live in and the art we make. Cultural leadership opportunities abound if artists think beyond the confines of traditional practices and existing infrastructure. Apart from the social good there is also employment and engagement potential for the plethora of unemployed artists out there.

Embedding artists in society and practice is more conducive to fulfilling our function. Peter Tregear in his Platform Paper *Enlightenment or Entitlement?* makes a strong argument for music training to be directly involved with the community, though he does not propose removing it from the university structure.[38]

Apprenticeship is a long-established practice in other trades, but it has been abandoned by the theatre and the responsibility has been surrendered to the tertiary education sector. But the university structure, with its emphasis on academic excellence and compliance is an inappropriate place for a budding actor or entrepreneur to learn the practicalities and opportunities of theatre life.

There are many more areas that require leadership but these three have strong cultural implications for the way we undertake our job as artists. They all require artists to step up and take on a greater role in laying out our values and purpose, taking responsibility for our future and seeking out different ways to achieve our goals.

Epilogue

There is a history of cultural leadership that we have forgotten about over the past few years, and cultural responsibility has been abrogated to government, universities, sponsors and stakeholders other than artists. Cultural leadership happens best when artists step up and wrestle the future, when we use our creative and imaginative powers to create alternate worlds that challenge and excite. Though I have continued to use theatre as my base for discussion here, the arts as a whole have to step into the ring and participate in the society we live in.

Australia is in need of a new breed of leaders who will show us the way to take responsibility for our Australian culture. Leaders who will persuade and coerce, act as political lightning rods for key issues and be articulate. Where will these leaders come from? Who are the cultural leaders we need? I know you can't force artistic directors to be more articulate advocates, but they can be questioned and supported by an active community of artists and audiences.

The 'Followship' that is needed is one of articulate and informed debate. Artistic directors are the ones in positions to show leadership. Artistic directorship is not just about the organisation, it is equivalent to being elected a member of an artistic parliament who represents an art form and its citizens. It is beholden on them to argue out ideas and challenge the hesitation to change.

We need to build a general trust in artists and our role in society and to challenge the erosion of the value of cultural expression, the kind of erosion that occurs when we artists abrogate our responsibilities and connections to our tribe, but also when the tribe forgets what the artist brings to our cultural wellbeing. We need to step up as artists for what we believe is important and show it through our work. Cultural leadership starts with artists being leaders.

It's a responsibility that starts with people like me.

Dear Australian Theatre Artists,

There are some choices to make: either get actively involved in imagining a future for our country or get out of the way.

If you can't articulate your work as a vision for a better, more humane society, then give it up.

If all you have to offer is beauty and distraction, work harder.

Share the stories of your successes and failures.

Use your imagination to think beyond what we have inherited to foresee what the future could be.

Look to the examples of those who have gone before us.

Aboriginal society has much to teach Australia in terms of how we treat our leaders, elders and wise people, how we define our role in a community and how we go about practising our culture.

Don't let gratitude interfere with your purpose.

Step up and take your place.

Thank you.

Love,
Wesley.

Endnotes may contain broken links. All hyperlinks were correct at the time of first publication.

1. Closing the Gap is a commitment endorsed by the Australian Government in March 2008, to reduce Indigenous disadvantage in life expectancy, child mortality, access to early childhood education, educational achievement and employment outcomes; to achieve Indigenous health equality within 25 years. http://www.healthinfonet.ecu.edu.au/closing-the-gap/key-facts/what-is-closing-the-gap.
2. Brendon Hills, 'Carbon Cate Blanchett tells Aussies to pay up over carbon charge'. *Sunday Telegraph.* May 29, 2013. http://www.dailytelegraph.com.au.
3. 'Sasquatch Music Festival 2009—Guy starts dance party'. *You Tube.* May 27, 2009. http://www.youtube.com/watch?v=GA8z7f7a2Pk.
4. Derek Sivers, 'How to start a movement', TED2010, *What the World Needs Now...,* Long Beach Performing Arts Centre, CA. February 10, 2010. *TED.* http://www.ted.com/talks/derek_sivers_how_to_start_a_movement.
5. Jörn Utzon was the architect who designed the Sydney Opera House. He controversially resigned in 1966 following a dispute with the NSW Government over work methods and costs. Other architects completed the building, which was opened in 1973.
6. Jim Sharman was artistic director of State Theatre Company of South Australia 1982–83. He established an ensemble and named it Lighthouse for this time and undertook radical interpretations of classics and new works. It was a short lived highlight of Australian theatre.
7. Peter Sellers is an internationally renowned director who was invited to be artistic director of the 2002 Adelaide Festival. Four months before the

opening he departed abruptly, under pressure from festival sources who lost faith in his unconventional way of programming.

8. Ashleigh Wilson, 'The audience holds the power'. *Australian*. March 20, 2013. http://www. theaustralian.com.au

9. Neil Armfield was co-artistic director of Nimrod in 1979 and artistic director of Belvoir 1994–2010; Alan Edwards was founding artistic director of Queensland Theatre Company 1970–88; Roger Hodgman was artistic director of Melbourne Theatre Company 1987–99; Aubrey Mellor was artistic director of Jane Street 1978-9, co-artistic direct Belvoir 1981–3 artistic director of Queensland Theatre Company 1988–93 and Playbox (now Malthouse) 1993–2004; Simon Phillips was artistic director of STCSA 1990–3 and MTC 2000-11; Andrew Ross was founding artistic director of Black Swan Theatre Company 1991–2003, director of Brisbane Powerhouse 2003-13; Jim Sharman was artistic director of Adelaide Festival 1982, and of STCSA/Lighthouse 1982–3; John Sumner was founding artistic director of Melbourne Theatre Company 1953–54 and 1959–87; Richard Wherrett was founding artistic director of Sydney Theatre Company 1979–89.

10. David Pledger, *Re-valuing the Artist in the New World Order,* Platform Papers no. 36, August 2014.

11. Jennifer Blocksidge was a respected actor, director and teacher and instrumental in the development of LaBoite in Brisbane. Rex Cramphorn (1941–91) was a theatre director, actor and reviewer originally from Brisbane, active in the 1970s and 80s and highly respected for his dramaturgy. Jack Davis (1917–2000) was an Aboriginal playwright, poet and activist, who wrote No Sugar and other classic plays of Indigenous urban life in the 1980s. Alma De Groen is a playwright and teacher whose plays were influential from the 1970s to 90s before she returned to her native New Zealand. Max Gillies is a prominent actor and satirist and founding member of the 1970s experimental theatre company Australian Performing Group. Louis

Nowra is a prolific and award-winning writer and playwright who first gained attention in the 1980s. His best-known play is Cosi Fan Tutte. John Romeril was a founding member of the Australian Performing Group and and has had long career as a playwright and activist. His best-known play is The Floating World. Stephen Sewell is a playwright of great social conscience who first came to attention in the 1980s; he is currently the head of playwriting at NIDA. Brian Syron (1934–93) was an Aboriginal performer, writer, director, teacher, who helped establish the Australian Playwrights Conference, Eora Arts Centre and Aboriginal National Theatre Trust. David Williamson is Australia's most popular playwright with over fifty produced plays since the late 1960s. Rod Wissler was artistic director of TN! in the 1980's and a celebrated actor, director and teacher. He recently retired as Dean of Creative Industries at QUT.

12. The Drama Committee was part of the Performing Arts Board of the Australia Council and assessed all drama applications including puppetry, circus, visual theatre, new form and hybrid performance. The structure changed in the late 1990s to create an autonomous Theatre Board.
13. Helen Nugent, *Securing the Future: inquiry into the major performing arts*, Department of Information Technology and the Arts, 1999. *Analysis and Policy Observatory*. https://apo.org.au/node/17634.
14. Richard Watts, 'Youth arts orgs lose out in funding cuts'. *Arts Hub*. News, November 1, 2013. www.artshub.com.au
15. Professor Emeritus Margaret Seares of the University of Western Australia is a prominent arts activist, a former Chair of the Australia Council and present Chair of the Perth International Arts Festival. John Garden-Gardiner is a noted dance teacher and historian, founder with his wife Alwyn of Earthly Delights, a dance teaching and advocacy organisation in Canberra.
16. Margaret Sears and John Gardiner-Garden, *Cultural Policies in Australia*, Australia Council, June 2011.

17. Hilary Glow and Katya Johanson, 'Looking for Cultural Value: critiques of Australian cultural policy'. *Asia Pacific Journal of Arts and Cultural Management*, Vol. 4, no. 2, December 2006, pp. 259-269. *Core Open Access Research Papers*, https://core.ac.uk/download/pdf/30686689.pdf.
18. *Arts for all Queenslanders Strategy 2014-2018*, Queensland Government, Department of Science, Information Technology and the Arts, Cabinet Documents, December 2013. *Queensland Government*. https://cabinet.qld.gov.au.
19. *Creative Nation, Commonwealth cultural policy,* Government of Australia, Department of Communications and the Arts, October, 1994, Preamble. Australian Policy and Observatory. https://apo.org.au.
20. 'Speech by the Prime Minister, the Hon P. J. Keating, MP', AWGIE Awards Presentation Dinner, Melbourne, July 10, 1992. *PM Transcripts*. Transcript ID: 8575. https://pmtranscripts.pmc.gov.au.
21. Former Treasurer Kim Beazley became Opposition Leader after the 1996 Election and was blamed for an $8 billion deficit by the Howard Government. It was nicknamed the Beazley Black Hole. 'Transcript of the Prime Minister, the Hon. John Howard, MP. Doorstop Interview—Sydney', 19 April, 1996. *PM Transcripts*. Transcript ID: 9980. https://pmtranscripts.pmc.gov.au.
22. *Creative Australia—National Cultural Policy*, Australian Government, Department of Infrastructure, Transport, Regional Development, Communication and the Arts. June 3, 2022, pp. 45-6.
23. Ben Eltham, 'Arts policy: where do Labor, the Coalition and the Greens stand?' *Guardian*. September 3, 2013. https://www.theguardian.com.
24. Raymond Gill, 'Budget cuts hit artists who can least afford it'. *Daily Review*. May 14, 2014. http://dailyreview.com.au.
25. 'Transfield holdings, Transfield Services, the Biennale of Sydney and the Transfield Foundation: A statement by Transfield Holdings addressing

inaccuracies in print and social media.' *Transfield.* https://www.transfield .com.au.

26. Pauline Peel is a cultural consultant and facilitator currently undertaking Australia Council funded research into Cultural Leadership in Communities. See http://www.paulinepeelconsulting.com.
27. Lyn Wallis: 'Opinion: Cultural Leadership in the Theatre', March 30, 2011. *Australia Council for the Arts.* https://australiacouncil.gov.au/news/speeches-and-opinions/opinion-cultural-leadership-in-the-theatre/
28. Katie Venner, 'Introduction' in *A Cultural Leadership Reader*, Sue Kay, Katie Venner, Susanne Burns and Mary Schwartz (eds), Cultural Leadership Program and Creative Choices, n.d. p. 5.
29. 'Australian Theatre Forum 2013 Wrap-up', 12 June 2013. *Australia Council for the Arts.* https://australiacouncil.gov.au/news/stories/australian-theatre-forum-2013-wrap-up.
30. ATF2013 'Delegate Feedback', 30 June 30, 2013. *Australian Theatre Forum.* http://www.australiantheatreforum.com.au/wp-content/uploads/2014/05/ATF2013_Delegate_Feedback.pdf.
31. Patrick Healy, 'Creating a supply chain of work by femail playwrights'. *New York Times*. June 16, 2014. http://www.nytimes.com.
32. The Clore Leadership Programme, UK, was established by the Clore Duffield Foundation on the initiative of the philanthropist Dame Vivien Duffield. It provides bursaries and mentorship with the aim of developing a generation of exceptional young leaders.
33. Robert Hewison, John Holden and Samuel Jones, *All Together: a creative approach to organisational change*, Demos, 2010. *Nesta.*https://www.nesta.org.uk
34. *Artistic Vibrancy: a way for organisations to talk about artistic impact*, Australia Council, e-book. https://www.australiacouncil.gov.au/ebook/artistic-vibrancy/publication/contents/pdfweb.pdf.
35. William Tate, quoted in *Kaospilot, Enterprising Leadership School of*

Social Change, Business Creativity and Personal Mastery, Curriculum, August 2013, Introduction, 4. *Docbox,* https://educationdocbox.com/Homework_and_Study_Tips/65814969-Kaospilot-enterprising-leadership.html#google_vignette.

36. 'The Project: The Magic Kombi' blog, http://magickombi.wordpress.com.
37. *Pursuit of Possible Planets,* Kaospilot Team 18, 2014. Final Exhibition catalogue. 2014. https://issuu.com/kaospilot/docs/kaospilot_graduates2014
38. Peter Tregear, *Enlightenment or Entitlement: Rethinking tertiary music education*, Platform Papers no. 39, February 2014.

About the author

Wesley Enoch AM is a Quandamooka man from Stradbroke Island. He is currently the Indigenous Chair in the Creative Industries at QUT. He has held the roles of Artistic Director at the Queensland Theatre Company, Ilbijerri and Kooemba Jdarra, Associate Artistic Director at Belvoir and Resident Director at Sydney Theatre Company and most recently Director of the Sydney Festival from 2017—2021. He has been a member of the Ethics Council of the National Congress of Australia's First Peoples, a board member of the Brisbane Indigenous Media Association, a Trustee of the Sydney Opera House, Chair of the First Nations Arts Panel of the Australia Council, Chair of the Create NSW Aboriginal Arts Board, a member of the Artistic Directorate of Hothouse Theatre and has facilitated numerous community consultations and forums.

His stage directing credits include *The 7 Stages of Grieving, The Sapphires, Stolen, The Sunshine Club, Nargun and the Stars, Parramatta Girls,* the Opening Ceremony of the 2006 and 2018 Commonwealth Games and *Black Diggers*. His writing credits include *The Story of the Miracles at Cookie's Table*, which won the 2006 Patrick White Playwrights Award, *The Sunshine Club, Black Medea, Grace* and *The 7 Stages of Grieving* (co-written with Deborah Mailman).

Wesley believes in the power of storytelling to affect people and change attitudes.

Submission to the Government on the National Cultural Policy

Julian Meyrick, Harriet Parsons, Stephen Sewell and the members of the Currency House Board and Editorial Committee

Gadigal country

Currency House is a not-for-profit organisation established by Katharine Brisbane, AM, the founder of Australia's leading performing arts publisher, Currency Press, in 2001. It promotes the engagement of artists in public affairs and publishes the long essay series Platform Papers by leaders in the performing arts, humanities, law and economics. Harriet Parsons took over the directorship of Currency House with Julian Meyrick, the General Editor of the New Platform Papers, in 2021. Sixty-three issues of Platform Papers were published from 2004–2021 and the second volume of the New Platform Papers is forthcoming in December. Currency House held its second annual Authors Convention in August, *From the Heart: the imperative for the arts,* to consider the implications of the Uluru Statement from the Heart for the National Cultural Policy.

Preamble

If we take our lead as a country from our First Nations, art is the expression of the values and spirituality of a people gathered together, and it is this important purpose that Australian artists engage in on a daily basis. As we reflect on who we are as Australians, we are guided by the bold conviction that it is through our art that we come to know ourselves. The profound truth of our species is that what guides us is not the search for simple existence, but the search for meaning that finds its expression in art and spirituality, without which existence has no value. Every nation has come to be, through the act of creating art and poetry, and none has survived their departure. If Australia wishes to be great, it must recognise the greatness of its artists and, by embracing their art, turn Australia into the kind of creative country everyone longs to live in.

We offer three recommendations for the government to consider in its consultation for a new National Cultural Policy, the primary one being a living wage for arts workers.

A Living Wage for Arts Workers

A living wage is the foundation of any economic sector, but this essential requirement has never been addressed in an Australian arts policy.

As largely itinerant workers, artists live insecure lives, and their willingness to work for love undercuts the principle of market competition. At the same time, the grants system was never intended to meet the ordinary needs of the sector as a whole, but to reward outstanding individuals. The standard of excellence sets the bar high, but the minimum standard, that recognises the majority, is missing. This minimum standard is essential to support the professionals—the 'jobbing actors', skilled technicians and administrators—who make the work of the stars possible.

The growing number of crises confronting the nation is demanding a new approach from government, that protects individuals by supporting their communities. A living wage for artists should be included among the measures the government is currently considering more generally for improving infrastructure, expanding services and increasing wages for low-income earners. The scheme for a living wage for artists proposed by Currency House is a non-inflationary measure for assisting low-income workers and increasing domestic productivity that puts 'First Nations first'.

The Arts Workers' Stipend

The Arts Workers Stipend is a job guarantee for arts workers. It is based on a proposal for a universal job guarantee put forward by

Noel Pearson which we will be publishing in the next volume of the New Platform Papers. A job guarantee makes the government the 'employer of last resort' and Pearson lists three economic benefits:

1. It lifts the income of the poorest Australians to a decent level.
2. It gives people all of the intangible personal, psychological and social benefits that come with work.
3. It achieves full employment without increasing inflation.

The job guarantee is non-inflationary, he explains, because 'it works as an automatic stabiliser in the economy: the pool of workers in the scheme rises and falls with the economic cycle. In a downturn the pool grows and when the labour market picks up the pool shrinks close to zero.'

The Arts Workers' Stipend (AWS) should be available to all arts workers, administered through the Australia Council and parallel the Australian Postgraduate Award (APA). Associating the AWA with the APA would link this new allowance to an existing standard.

Importantly the APA is tax free. An AWS of the same amount—$24,653 in 2022—would therefore allow an individual arts practitioner to earn a further $21,884 before they begin paying tax. This would equate to a gross income of approximately $50,000 per year—i.e. a low-level professional salary. The use of tax offsets would allow the government to provide significant financial support to arts workers via a relatively modest stipend.

Administration of the AWS

The Australia Council's application processes are familiar to arts workers and involve well-established systems of peer review. Awarding the stipend would follow the APA model, with applicants approved in three stages:

Stage 1: Acceptance of the initial application. CV, portfolio and references. The entry phase would set a low bar and establish the applicants' track record as a cultural practitioner. We recommend that, in addition to applications from arts workers directly, the Council also accept applications from groups on behalf of arts workers who are making a significant contribution to their community.

Stage 2: Confirmation after one year. A closer examination of the applicants' work and their contribution to the arts sector, their community or peer group.

Stage 3: Permanent acceptance into the scheme after five years. The final phase would show which applicants had established a permanent career in the arts and were in need of a permanent stipend, while those who withdraw will not be disadvantaged by their years of contribution to the arts. The stipend could be increased at this stage to allow arts workers to give up employment in sectors not related to their creative practice.

Peer Review. Peer assessment over five years provides an effective protection against fraud, with references and recommendations from communities providing further safeguards that are also supportive of the applicant.

Phasing in. This program would be phased in gradually because it requires recipients to apply for the stipend. It could be regulated further by capping the number of new stipends offered each year.

First Nations First

The Arts Workers' Stipend would be especially important for Aboriginal artists who produce Australia's highest arts export earnings. At the recent Currency House convention, APY artist Sally Scales described shocking exploitation of Aboriginal artists who have been trapped into financial slavery by unscrupulous dealers through debt obligations that can never be repaid. The economic autonomy provided by a stipend could prevent Aboriginal artists from falling into this trap, while benefitting the community as a whole by supporting a career path that strengthens the connection to culture. The AWS would effectively be placing 'First Nations first' by allowing Aboriginal communities to capitalise on their commercial success and provide cultural leadership to the nation through the autonomous voice of their artists.

Other Recommendations

An end to the 'efficiency dividend'

Our second recommendation is the immediate cessation of the imposition of efficiency dividends on the budgets of cultural and creative institutions. These no longer promote efficiency (if they ever did) nor do they produce a dividend. Reducing budgets and shortening production times as a regular administrative practice leads to poor outcomes. Over time, it cripples the institutions to which these regressive measures are applied.

Return to Collegiality

Our final recommendation is for a return to collegiality in relations between the arts and government. We would like to see the Minister and Office of the Arts staff prioritise the development of congenial relationships with artists and arts organisations and characterise the arts as a humanising sector in our economy, rather than an underperforming 'industry' in all government communications; promoting the arts by using Australian actors, designers and directors in its messaging and as an instrument of 'soft diplomacy' internationally, including its Indigenous Foreign Policy; employing arts workers in government arts bureaucracy, particularly at the Australia Council; and restoring the arm's length status of the Australia Council as a mark of trust.

Conclusion

We commend the Minister for conducting the consultation, and strongly support the development of a National Cultural Policy. Measures to strengthen the work of cultural practitioners and institutions need not be complex. Simple initiatives aimed at improving the basic income of artists and the tone of government relations are achievable. In respect of an Arts Workers stipend, Currency House has spent considerable time developing this important potential policy initiative.

We would be pleased to assist the government in consulting on it further, including drawing on our wide range of authors and supporters in the arts and cultural sector.

List of Platform Papers

Platform Papers

First published July 2004

PP1 *'Our ABC'—A Dying Culture?* Martin Harrison

PP2 *Survival of the Fittest: The artist versus the corporate world*, Christopher Latham

2005

PP3 *Trapped by the Past: Why our theatre is facing paralysis*, Julian Meyrick

PP4 *The Myth of the Mainstream: Politics and the performing arts in Australia today*, Robyn Archer

PP5 *Shooting Through: Australian film and the brain drain*, Storry Walton

PP6 *Art in a Cold Climate: Rethinking the Australia Council*, Keith Gallasch

2006

PP7 *Does Australia Need a Cultural Policy?* David Throsby

PP8 *Body for Hire? The state of dance in Australia*, Amanda Card

PP9 *What Price a Creative Economy?* Stuart Cunningham

PP10 *Satire—or Sedition? The threat to national insecurity*, Jonathan Biggins

2007

PP11 *A Regional State of Mind: Making art outside metropolitan Australia*, Lyndon Terracini

PP12 *Film in the Age of Digital Distribution: The challenge for Australian content*, Richard Harris

PP13 *Cross-racial Casting: Changing the face of Australian theatre*, Lee Lewis

PP14 *Who Profits from the Arts? Taking the measure of culture*, Kay Ferres and David Adair

2008

P15 *A Sustainable Arts Sector: What will it take?* Cathy Hunt and Phyllida Shaw

PP16 *The Permanent Underground: Australian contemporary jazz in the new Millennium*, Peter Rechniewski

PP17 *What is an Australian Play? Have we failed our ethnic writers?* Chris Mead

PP18 *Getting Heard: Achieving an effective arts advocacy*, Chris Puplick

2009

PP19 *'Your Genre is Black': Indigenous performing arts and policy* Hilary Glow and Katya Johanson

PP20 *Beethoven or Britney: The great divide in music education*, Robert Walker

PP21 *Television: What will rate in the new tomorrow?* Ian David

PP22 *Copyright, Collaboration and the future of dramatic authorship*, Brent Salter

2010 (one paper cancelled)

PP23 *Whatever Happened to the STC Actors Company?* James Waites

PP24 *The Digital Playing Fields: New rulz for film art and performance*, Shilo McClean

PP25 *Moving Across Disciplines: Dance in the twenty-first century*, Erin Brannigan

2011

PP26 *Not Just an Audience: Young people transforming our theatre*, Lenine Bourke and Mary Ann Hunter

PP27 *Hello, World! Promoting the arts on the web*, Robert Reid

PP28 *The Fall and Rise of the VCA*, Richard Murphet

PP29 *Democracy versus Creativity in Australian Classical Music*, Nicole Canham

2012

P30 *Indig-curious: Who can play Aboriginal roles?* Jane Harrison

PP31 *Finding a place on the Asian stage*, Alison Carroll and Carrillo Gantner

PP32 *History is Made at Night: Live music in Australia*, Clinton Walker

PP33 *Changing Times at NIDA*, Chris Puplick

2013

PP34 *It's Culture, Stupid! Reflections of an arts bureaucrat*, Leigh Tabrett

PP35 *The Music of Place: Reclaiming the practice*, Jon Rose

PP 36 *Re-valuing the Artist in the New World Order*, David Pledger

PP37 *Not at a Cinema Near You: Australia's film distribution problem*, Lauren Carroll Harris

2014

PP38 *Enlightenment or Entitlement? Rethinking tertiary music education*, Peter Tregear

PP39 *The Retreat of our National Drama*, Julian Meyrick

PP40 *Take Me to Your Leader: The dilemma of cultural leadership*, Wesley Enoch

PP41 *Education and the arts: Creativity in the promised new order*, Meg Upton with Naomi Edwards

2015

PP42 *The Time Is Ripe for the Great Australian Musical*, John Senczuk

PP43 *The Arts and the Common Good*, Katharine Brisbane

PP44 *Cultural Precincts: Art or commodity?* Justin Macdonnell

PP45 *Paying the Piper: There has to be another way*, Cathy Hunt

2016

PP46 *The Designer: Decorator or dramaturg?* Stephen Curtis

PP47 *Why We Need a Cultural Economy*, Justin O'Connor

PP48 *When the Goal Posts Move*, Ben Eltham

PP49 *The Lighting Designer: What is 'good' lighting*, Nigel Levings

2017

PP50 *Restless Giant: Changing cultural values in regional Australia*, Lindy Hume

PP51 *Missing in Action: The ABC and Australia's screen culture*, Kim Dalton

PP52 *Putting Words in their Mouths: The playwright and screenwriter at work*, Andrew Bovell

PP53 *The Jobbing Actor: Rules of engagement*, Lex Marinos

2018

PP54 *Young People and the Arts: An agenda for change*, Sue Giles

PP55 *Art, Politics, Money: Revisiting Australia's cultural policy*, David Throsby

PP56 *Falling Through the Gaps: Our artists' health and welfare*, Mark RW Williams

PP57 *Cultural Justice and the right to thrive*, Scott Rankin

2019

PP58 *The Changing Landscape of Australian Documentary*, Tom Zubrycki

PP59 *Ngarra-Burria: New music and the search for an Australian sound*, Christopher Sainsbury

PP60 *Capturing the Vanishing; A choreographer and film*, Sue Healey

PP61 *Criticism, Performance and the need for conversation*, Alison Croggon

2020

PP62 *Performing Arts Markets and their Conundrums*, Justin Macdonnell

2021

PP63 *On the Lessons of History*, Katharine Brisbane

The New Platform Papers

2021

Vol. 1 *What Future for the Arts in a post-Pandemic World?*

Foreword by Julian Meyrick

Season's Greetings from Katharine Brisbane

No. 1 *Imagininaton in the Arts and Economics: papers from the inaugural Platform Papers Authors Convention*

'Introduction: A Snail May Put His Horns Out', Harriet Parsons

'Models, Uncertainty and Imagination in Economics', Richard Bronk

'What's Wrong with Cannibalism?' Jonathan Biggins and John Quggin,

'The Fable of the Bees' (1714), Bernard Mandeville

'A Modest Proposal' (1729), Jonathan Swift

Astrid Jorgensen, 'You Can Sing (Averagely)!'

PP63 *On the Lessons of History,* Katharine Brisbane (2021 reprint)

CURRENCY HOUSE INC.

Currency House is a not-for-profit organisation devoted to promoting wider understanding of the work of artists and creative practitioners and how it contributes to Australia's social and political life.

currencyhouse.org.au

ISBN: 978-1-922762-54-2
ISSN: 2653-3308

Correspondence should be addressed to:
The Editor
The New Platform Papers
P. O. Box 2270
Strawberry Hills NSW 2012 Australia
Email: editor@currencyhouse.org.au

Typeset in Garamond.
Printed in Australia by Ligare Book Printers, Riverwood.
The paper used to produce this book comes from wood grown in sustainable forests.